MW01015424

PACKS ON!

Memoirs of the 10th Mountain Division in World War II

A. B. Feuer

Foreword by Senator Bob Dole

STACKPOLE BOOKS

0 11557 03289 5

Copyright © 2004 by A. B. Feuer

Published in paperback in 2006 by
STACKPOLE BOOKS
5067 Ritter Road
Mechanicsburg, PA 17055
www.stackpolebooks.com

"PACKS ON!" MEMOIRS OF THE 10TH MOUNTAIN DIVISION, by A. B. Feuer,
was originally published in hard cover by Praeger, an imprint of Greenwood Publishing Group, Inc., Westport, CT. Copyright © 2004 by A. B. Feuer. Paperback edition by arrangement with Greenwood Publishing Group, Inc. All rights reserved.

Printed in the United States of America

10 9 8 7 6 5 4 3 2 1

FIRST EDITION

ISBN 0-8117-3289-4 (Stackpole paperback)
ISBN 978-0-8117-3289-5 (Stackpole paperback)

The Library of Congress has cataloged the hardcover edition as follows:

Feuer, A. B., 1925–
    Packs on! : memoirs of the 10th Mountain Division / A. B. Feuer; foreword by
Bob Dole
        p. cm.
    ISBN 0-275-97784-6
    1. United States. Army. Mountain Division, 10th—History. 2. World War,
1939–1945—Regimental histories—United States. 3. World War, 1939–1945—
Campaigns—Italy. 4. World War, 1939–1945—Personal narratives, America. 5.
Mountain warfare—History—20th century. I. Title.
    D769.310th.F48   2004
    940.54'215—dc22   2004053191

Contents

Foreword by Senator Bob Dole   iv

Acknowledgments   v

10th Mountain Division   vi

Timeline   vii

Map Section   xi

1. Introduction   1

2. German Ski Troops: Training and Tactics   7

3. The 87th Mountain Infantry Regiment: The Kiska Campaign   19

4. Camps Hale and Swift: Prelude to Italy   30

5. The 86th Mountain Infantry Regiment: The Italian Campaign   32

6. The 85th Mountain Infantry Regiment: The Italian Campaign   59

7. The 87th Mountain Infantry Regiment: The Italian Campaign   81

8. The 110th Mountain Signal Company: The Italian Campaign   104

9. Company D, 126th Mountain Engineer Battalion:
   The Italian Campaign   113

10. The 10th Mountain Cavalry Reconnaissance Troop:
    The Italian Campaign   139

11. The Diary of a German Soldier   141

12. The Italian Campaign: A German Retrospect   144

13. Epilogue   149

References   150

Index   152

Photo essay follows page 58

Foreword

European countries have always considered their ski and mountain troops as elite infantry units. When America entered World War II, it became evident that if the United States was going to wage a successful war in Europe, it would have to defeat the enemy's finest soldiers.

However, the U.S. Army was deficient in one important respect: it did not have a mountain division. Charles Minot Dole, founder of the National Ski Patrol, realized that we would be fighting the enemy on his own turf—and that included mountainous terrain. Dole urged President Franklin Roosevelt and General George Marshall to form a specially trained mountain unit. Dole stated, "It is more reasonable to make soldiers out of skiers than skiers out of soldiers."

On July 15, 1943, the 10th Mountain Division was activated at Camp Hale, Colorado, as an all-civilian volunteer division. Although skiing skills were desired, qualifications were broad enough to include all types of outdoorsmen—including cowboys, forest rangers, and woodsmen.

Recruits with skiing experience were accepted from many eastern colleges and prep schools. World class skiers such as Torger Tokle, Robert Livermore, and Werner von Trapp joined the division.

In order to fill out the 10th's complement of fifteen thousand men, draftees and soldiers from other units were also assigned to the new organization. The 10th Mountain was probably the smartest and best educated division in the army, before I arrived, and scored the highest on U.S. Army tests and qualifications for officer candidate school. This resourcefulness came in handy as the 10th Mountain boys battled the veteran Alpine troops of German Field Marshall Albert Kesselring.

God Bless America,
Bob Dole
March 19, 2003

Acknowledgments

I would like to thank Senator Bob Dole for his Foreword to this manuscript and retired District Judge James P. Brice for his expertise. I would also like to recognize Audrey Wendland for the untold hours and e-mails she devoted to this project. And thanks are also due to the many members of the 10th Mountain Division Association who sent in their stories.

Unfortunately, due to the heavy volume of letters received, it was impossible to use every submission. But there may be another book about the 10th Mountain Division at a later date.

10th Mountain Division

* * *

Major General George P. Hays
Division Commander

Brigadier General Robinson E. Duff
Assistant Division Commander

Brigadier General David L. Ruffner
Division Artillery Commander

Colonel Earl F. Thomson
Chief of Staff

* * *

85th Mountain Infantry Regiment
86th Mountain Infantry Regiment
87th Mountain Infantry Regiment
604 Field Artillery Battalion
605 Field Artillery Battalion
616 Field Artillery Battalion
10th Mountain Anti-tank Battalion
10th Mountain Quartermaster Battalion
10th Mountain Medical Battalion
10th Mountain Cavalry Reconnaissance Troop
126th Mountain Engineer Battalion
710th Mountain Ordnance Company
110th Mountain Signal Company
10th Mountain Military Police Platoon
Headquarters, 10th Mountain Division
Headquarters, 10th Mountain Division Artillery

Timeline

10th Mountain Division
Italian Campaign

December 11, 1944
The 86th Regiment departed Camp Patrick Henry, Virginia, and boarded the U.S.S. *Argentina*. The ship arrived at Naples, Italy, on December 22.

January 4, 1945
The 85th and 87th Regiments left Hampton Roads, Virginia, aboard the U.S.S. *West Point*.

January 8, 1945
The 86th Regiment moved to the front lines north of Bagni di Lucca near Mount Belvedere.

January 9, 1945
General George P. Hays, commanding the 10th Mountain Division, arrived at Naples, Italy. After conferring with General Lucian K. Truscott, Jr., commander of the U.S. Fifth Army Corps, a plan was formulated to capture Mount Belvedere and all the high ground east of the town of Tole. Mount Belvedere provided the enemy with a clear view of one of the main approaches to the Po Valley. Hays realized that an attack on Belvedere could only be successful if German positions on Riva Ridge, which overlooked Belvedere, was taken.

January 13, 1945
The *West Point* with the 85th and 87th Regiments aboard docked at Naples, Italy.

January 14, 1945

Companies of the 85th Regiment embarked aboard LCIs (Landing Craft Infantry) for a trip up the coast to Leghorn, then by truck to Pisa. Troops of the 87th reached Pisa by rail, while others boarded the Italian freighter *Sestriere* for the voyage to Leghorn and then trucked to Pisa.

January 20, 1945

All three 10th Mountain Division regiments moved close to the front lines near Mount Belvedere. Colonel Raymond C. Barlow commanded the 85th Regiment, Colonel Clarence M. Tomlinson the 86th, and Colonel David M. Fowler the 87th. For about a month the ski troops familiarized themselves with the terrain by conducting reconnaissance and combat patrols.

February 16, 1945

General Hays planned to use the entire 10th Mountain Division plus artillery, armor, and air power for an attack on Riva Ridge, Mount Belvedere, and Mount Gorgolesco.

February 18, 1945

At dark, more than seven hundred men of the 86th Regiment made a daring climb and successful assault on Riva Ridge. Within two days, men of Company D, 126th Mountain Engineer Battalion, had erected an aerial tramway to evacuate wounded and deliver supplies.

February 20, 1945

The Second Battalion of the 85th Regiment launched its assault on Mount della Torraccia. But because of fierce enemy counterattacks, the position was not secured until February 24.

March 5, 1945

The 87th Regiment captured Castel d'Aiano while the 85th seized Mount della Spe. This cut the main German line of communications and supply to the Po Valley. The stage was now set for the coming Spring offensive.

April 14, 1945

On the first day of the offensive, the 10th Mountain Division attacked German positions north of Mount della Spe. On the left flank, the 85th Regiment captured Hills 909 and 913. At the center, the 87th assaulted Torre Iussi, while on the right flank, the 86th Regiment stormed Rocca Roffeno.

April 17, 1945

The 87th Regiment broke through the German defenses and captured Tole. This enabled the 10th Mountain Division to operate on a terrain of gentle slopes that descended gradually into the Po Valley.

April 20, 1945
The 85th Regiment advanced rapidly toward Bologna. General Hays formed a task force to spearhead the drive north to the Po River.

April 22, 1945
The Third Battalion of the 85th was assigned the mission to lead the dash to the Po and seize a location for crossing the river.

April 23, 1945
About 1 A.M., the task force reached San Benedetto near the banks of the Po, and a defense perimeter was established. At noon, the First Battalion of the 87th Regiment crossed the river under fire. Company D of the 126th Mountain Engineer Battalion manned the assault boats. By night-fall, the 85th Regiment had also crossed the Po.

April 24, 1945
The 86th Regiment crossed the river as the 10th Mountain Division expanded its bridgehead and reconnoitered the routes north.

April 25, 1945
A task force commanded by Colonel William O. Darby was given the mission of capturing Verona. Darby's troops entered Verona the following day only to find that elements of the 85th Division had already captured the town and silenced most of the enemy opposition. By evening, Darby's fast-moving task force had seized Lazise, a town on the east shore of Lake Garda.

April 30, 1945
While 10th Mountain troops were attacking the town of Torbole, an exploding enemy artillery shell killed Colonel Darby. On the same day, an 85th Regiment assault force crossed Lake Garda in DUKWs, amphibious craft nicknamed "ducks."

May 2, 1945
The German Army in Italy surrenders.

May 4, 1945
Racing rapidly north, the Third Battalion of the 86th Regiment reached the Alps on the border between Italy and Austria.

May 7, 1945
Germany surrendered.

May 20, 1945
The 10th Mountain Division reached Udine in northeastern Italy. Its mission was to join troops of the British Eighth Army and prevent further westward movement by Yugoslav forces.

July 14, 1945
The 10th Mountain Division was ordered to return to the United States for further training in preparation for the invasion of Japan. Plans called for the division to attack Kyushu on November 2, 1945.

August 6, 1945
An atomic bomb was dropped on Hiroshima, Japan.

August 9, 1945
A second atomic bomb was dropped on Nagasaki, Japan.

August 15, 1945
Japan surrenders.

September 15, 1945
The troops of the 10th Mountain Division return to Camp Carson, Colorado, after thirty-day furloughs.

November 30, 1945
The 10th Mountain Division is inactivated.

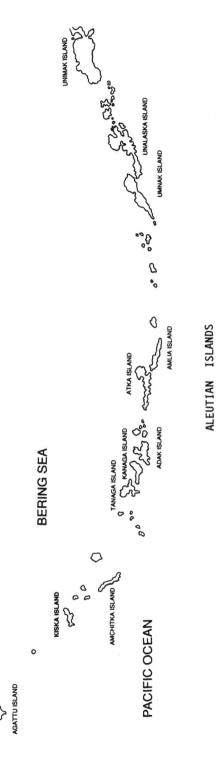

The Alaska Theater: The Kiska Campaign

Italy

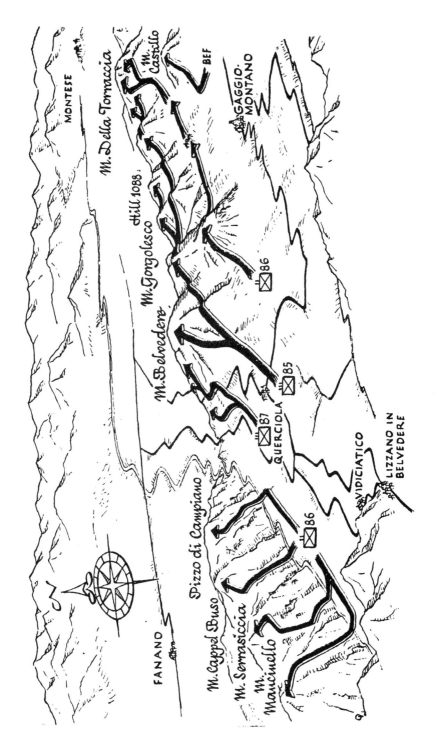

Riva Ridge—M. Belvedere—M. Della Torraccia

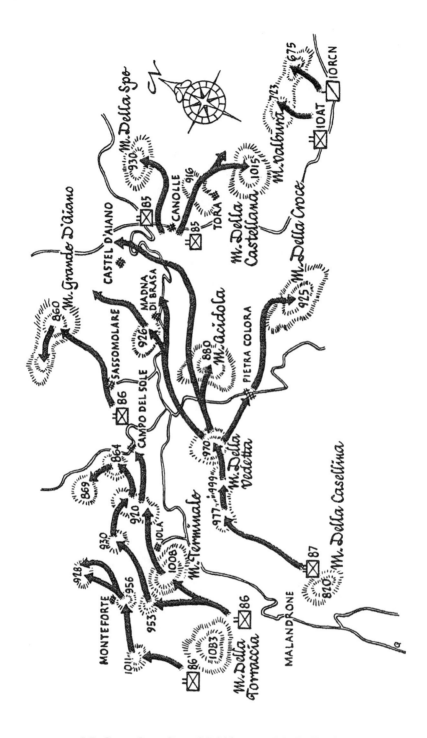

M. Grande—Castel D'Aiano—M. Della Spe

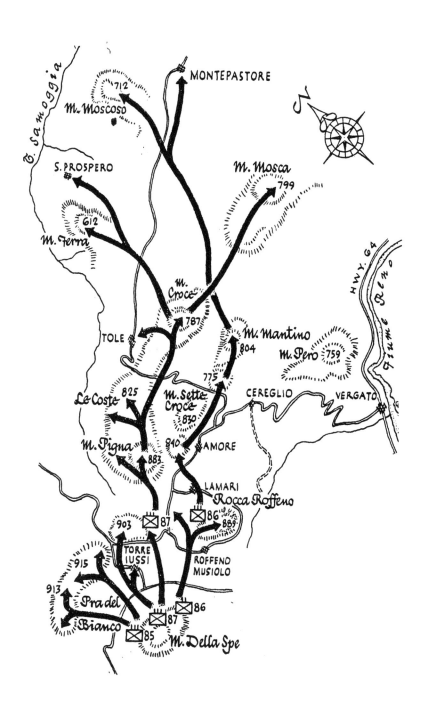

Initial Attack

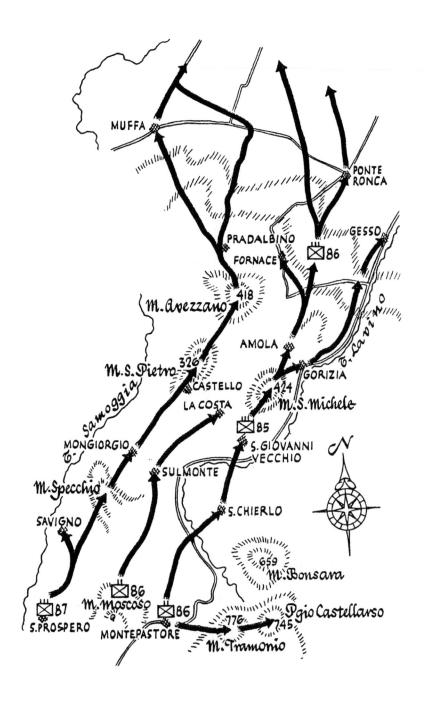

Exploitation

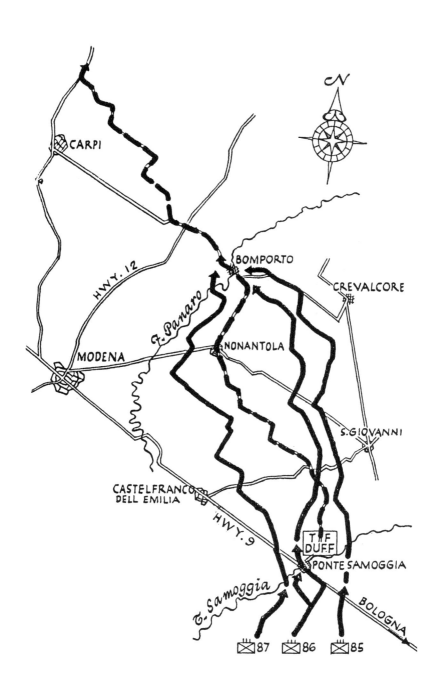

Pursuit in the Po Valley

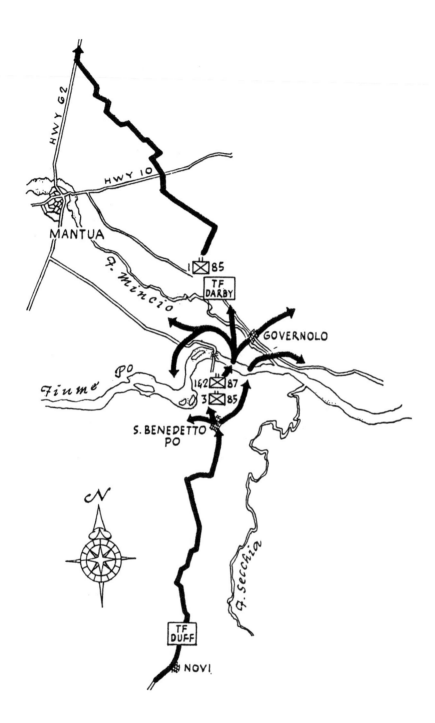

The Po River Crossing

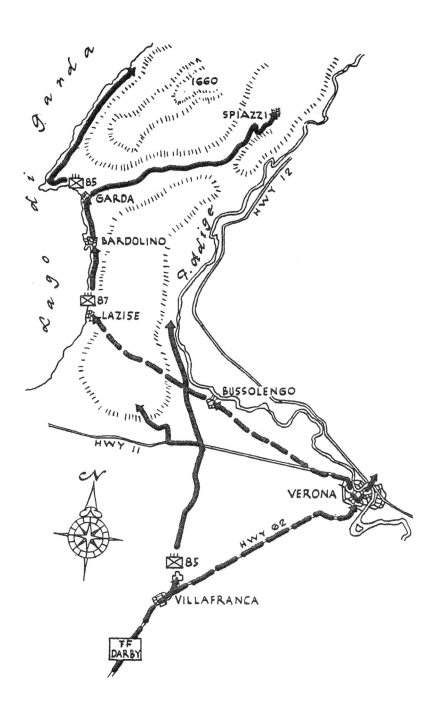

Into the Alps

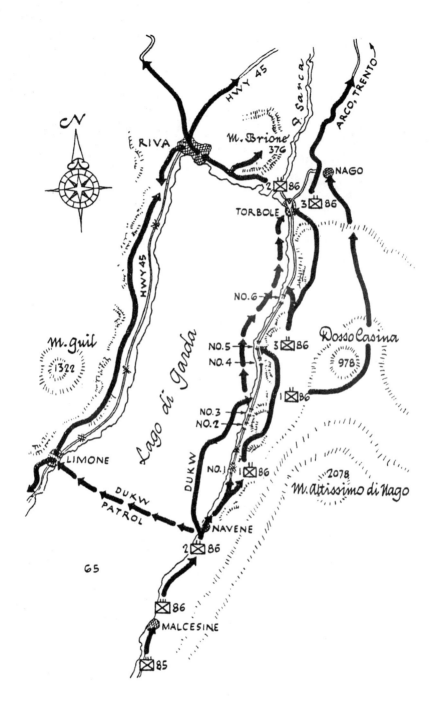

Lake Garda—The Final Battles

CHAPTER 1

Introduction

For several years prior to the outbreak of World War II in September 1939, many foreign armies had established mountain divisions. These troops were trained to fight in the cold and snow of high altitudes.

Countries such as Finland, Russia, Germany, Norway, France, and Italy were among the first nations to create military organizations that specialized in winter warfare. The United States, however, did not have a single mountain division to put in the field.

During the 1930s—while Europe was frantically arming itself for the coming conflict—the American public felt comfortable and safe behind three thousand miles of water to the east and eight thousand miles of ocean to the west. But the Japanese attack on Pearl Harbor, on December 7, 1941, was a wake-up call to America's vulnerability.

Six months later, pressing her advantage, Japan sent a naval task force to occupy two islands in the Aleutian chain. On June 6, 1942, approximately twelve hundred soldiers landed on Kiska, while another twelve hundred went ashore on Attu. Not until four days later did the U.S. Navy patrol plane discover the enemy force.

During the winter of 1942, American submarines and aircraft blockaded Attu and Kiska to prevent the Japanese from resupplying their troops. To further isolate the enemy, U.S. Army detachments occupied Adak and Amchitka, and airfields were quickly constructed on the islands.

But the U.S. high command also realized that it needed men trained in winter and mountain warfare, and the 87th Mountain Infantry Battalion was formed at Fort Lewis, Washington. The organization was composed of volunteers from the 3rd, 41st, and 44th Divisions, plus civilians recruited by the National Ski Patrol System. The men trained at Mount Ranier, Washington. But the location was not suited for the training of soldiers in all phases of mountain combat.

The main accomplishment at Ranier was instruction in the technique of military skiing. The mountain soldier not only had to be familiar with downhill runs but also cross-country skiing, both while carrying a heavy pack.

Tests were also conducted as to the relative value of snowshoes and skis. Snowshoes were found to be superior where heavy equipment had to be carried. But for a surprise attack, or fast-moving cross-country operations, skis were more efficient.

A steady stream of volunteers soon began applying for mountain training, and the 87th Battalion rapidly became a regiment. In September 1942, a mountain training center was activated at Camp Carson, Colorado. And, two months later, the center was moved to a newly completed facility at Camp Hale, Colorado.

While at Camp Hale, the men were instructed in special mountaineering methods, at the same time learning to use the different weapons and other equipment.

During the winter of 1942–1943, it became evident that a tactical unit as large as a division could be organized and trained for mountain and cold-weather operations. A few months later, the 10th Light Division (Alpine) was activated. Three infantry regiments were formed—the 85th, 86th, and 90th.

Meanwhile, in mid-1943, the 87th Regiment was transferred to the Alaskan Defense Command.

On May 11, 1943, about ten thousand men of the U.S. 7th Infantry Division landed on Attu. After a bitter eighteen-day battle, the Japanese force was wiped out. American losses were also heavy, with six hundred men killed and twelve hundred wounded.

After the loss of Attu, the Japanese decided to evacuate their troops from Kiska. Taking advantage of heavy fog to cover its approach, an enemy task force consisting of two cruisers and six destroyers successfully rescued the garrison and returned to its base in the Kurile Islands.

The Japanese withdrawal from Kiska was accomplished without being observed by American ships or aircraft. Believing that enemy soldiers were still on the island, the U.S. Army planned to launch an amphibious assault on Kiska. A large invasion force was assembled. In late July, ships carrying thirty-four thousand men, including the 87th Infantry Regiment, sailed for the Aleutians.

The task force arrived off Kiska on the morning of August 15. A heavy mist and creeping fog shrouded the island. The troops landed without incident. But the Americans, expecting strong resistance, began shooting at every sound and shadow. Soldiers became disoriented and fired at their own men. Others became victims of mines and booby traps. By the time cooler heads prevailed, the 87th Regiment itself had suffered twenty-three men killed and fifty-five wounded.

Upon returning to the United States, the 87th rejoined the 10th Light Division, and the 90th Regiment was transferred to another command. The mountain division now comprised the 85th, 86th, and 87th Infantry Regiments. A number of the 87th veterans of the Kiska campaign were transferred to the other two regiments.

Specialized winter warfare training now became intense. The men of the 10th Light Division were instructed in rock climbing, scouting, map reading, use of the compass, communications, and record keeping.

The final phase of the training was restricted to the movement of troops along a seven-mile route, ending with a climb of two thousand feet to a bivouac.

About halfway up the rugged slope, an area was cleared for unloading carts and packing supplies aboard mules. From this point, the climb became difficult. It took the troops eighteen hours to reach the bivouac. The reason for the slow advance was that the mules kept slipping on the ice and had to be continually repacked.

The officers and men of the 10th were primarily concerned with training, while tactics were relegated to a minor role until the troops became proficient in operating under winter conditions.

Certain fundamentals of mountain warfare already existed and had been used by foreign countries for many years. Basically, they included a few cardinal rules: Seize and hold the ridges, and you command the valleys. Strike with speed and deception at the enemy's lines of communication and supply, and prevent him from taking the passes.

The Mountain Training Center did not develop any tactics of its own. The standard flatland infantry tactics were employed and converted to high-altitude operations. This adaptation was not always successful, but there was no manual available for use as a guide.

Many officers of the 10th Light Division were sent to the Infantry School at Fort Benning, Georgia, and the Command and General Staff School at Fort Leavenworth, Kansas. Although little emphasis was placed on conducting operations on difficult terrain, the basic principles, when applied to mountain and winter warfare, were valid.

The unit proficiency tests, however, were based on the assumption that friendly forces held the ridges and were able to maneuver safely in the valleys. But the soldiers of the 10th were well cognizant of the fact that "He who holds the ridges is master of all below."

Camouflage was the most important factor when fighting on snow-covered ground. Although equipment could be whitened to blend in with the landscape, ski tracks were easy to spot from the air.

White clothing also had its disadvantages when units were operating in timber areas. Whether it was more important to wear white to blend in with the snow or olive drab to escape detection among the trees was arguable.

Another decision was the building of warming fires. Usually, the company commander determined if his men were in more danger from freezing than from enemy artillery or air bombardment.

Night maneuvers and missions became a prime training objective. Many of the men, however, had not reached that proficiency. In fact, it was difficult enough for them to learn daylight maneuvers. But it was at night when the ghostly white camouflage proved most effective, and the silent movement on soft snow was the main element of a surprise attack. Very dark nights proved to be the best time to travel across snow and dangerous ice.

A soldier's footing was firm and safe during darkness when the ground was frozen, and the danger of rock or snow avalanches were at a minimum. But, for the most part, the Mountain Training Center continued to specialize in daylight operations. The tactics of mountain and winter warfare were still kept subordinated to the training process.

One constant problem was the resupplying of troops in mountainous areas. Despite using snow vehicles and mules to transport provisions and ammunition, eventually all supplies reached a place where they had to be backpacked by the men themselves. The 10th Light Division did not have the luxury of porters as used by several European armies. Supplying troops by air was believed to be the answer.

During the 1943 maneuvers at Camp Hale, two C-47 transports flew three missions to resupply a mountain battalion. On the first flight, thirty-two cartons were dropped by parachute. Sixteen were recovered, but the others landed on a dangerous slope and were not retrieved. A second mission was sent out to replace the loads that were not salvaged. The third flight was made to test the possibility of dropping supplies into deep snow without using parachutes. The soft blanket of snow provided excellent cushioning, and most of the items were recovered in good condition. However, lack of communications between air and ground units, plus inclement weather, prevented more extensive air-drop missions.

Throughout these experiments, the problem of radio operation in mountainous terrain remained a dilemma. Signal panels were used only once, and then just in the shape of an arrow.

After results of the C-47 missions had been studied, the army concluded that supplying mountain troops by air was practical, but with limitations. The air force recommended that visibility should be at least two miles, and with ceilings high enough for safe navigation in valleys and passes. The weather should also be clear with moderate wind velocities.

Another suggestion was made that a system be established whereby aircraft could deliver the immediate needs of a ski unit. This would prevent dropping supplies that were already on hand.

Throughout their training period, the mountain troops struggled continuously with the weight of eighty-five-pound packs. Wherever vehicles and mules could not be used, every item of equipment and provisions had to be carried on the backs of the soldiers themselves.

Attempts were made to correct the problem. The weight of sleeping bags was reduced from twelve to nine pounds, and gasoline stoves from three pounds to one pound. Heavy manila climbing ropes were replaced by lightweight nylon cable. Dehydrated rations also saved on the load each ski trooper had to carry.

But there was no immediate solution to one pressing predicament. Tents were very heavy because they were waterproofed. A two-man tent weighed thirteen pounds. The men preferred to build lean-tos or snow caves, or just unroll their sleeping bags on the cold ground.

One detail in particular distinguished a ski troop regiment from a regular infantry outfit: specialization. Right from the beginning, the Mountain Training Center suffered from lack of adequate communication with army headquarters. There were a few reasons for this. One particular point was the fact that both mountaineering and skiing were unfamiliar to American military tacticians. Another was that nearly all the technical skills and experience of the mountain regiments were to be found among the volunteer enlisted men. In 1941, the highest ranking officer with a skiing background was a captain.

The soldiers of the 10th Mountain Light Division included many world-famous skiers and mountaineers. Among the prominent volunteers were Walter Prager, Peter Gabriel, Torger Tokle, and a host of others. But these experts made up only about 20 percent of the division. The majority of the men were assigned through regular army channels. Some of these soldiers, however, were not qualified and did not measure up to the rugged standards required of mountain troops.

Men either loved the life of a mountain soldier, and strove hard to develop their skills, or took no interest in the training whatsoever. The latter would point out that they had not asked to be assigned to the 10th and directed all their energy toward effecting a transfer to a more pleasant and less arduous assignment.

One reason for the mistakes in recruiting men for the mountain division was that the Department of the Army did not realize the highly specialized requirements of ski troops or the training involved. In addition, no physical standards had been established for a division of this kind. As a result, anyone who could pass the customary army physical exam could find himself assigned to a mountain regiment. Moreover, when the directive was issued authorizing the transfer of men to the 10th Light Division, many commanding officers used the opportunity to get rid of any troublemakers.

Another aggravating situation was the difficulty in obtaining officer ratings for the ski and mountaineering instructors. This usually resulted in army privates teaching officers the intricate fundamentals of military skiing.

As the fledgling mountain division's troubles continued, the morale of the instructors, and the state of training itself, began to suffer. This was mainly due to the fact that U.S. Army Headquarters was slow to recognize the need for trained mountain personnel and then, when it finally had them, proceeded to penalize the very men who were needed to develop the organization into a skilled fighting unit.

The army high command had decided that there was no urgent need for mountain troops and that the existing training program was satisfactory. The program would have been adequate if it had been carried out effectively. But the army continued to favor standard infantry training at the expense of specialization. The 10th Light Division was considered an experiment.

CHAPTER 2

German Ski Troops: Training and Tactics

In 1939, the German Army was a formidable force, especially since it had no real competition. However, the author, in an interview with the late Major General John F. Ruggles, 22nd U.S. Infantry Regiment, described a different kind of enemy—with excellent, intelligent soldiers but hampered by a World War I mentality of using horse-drawn carts to transport food, ammunition, and gasoline.

This fact became very evident by photographs—taken early in the war by the Germans themselves—and carefully studied by the Allied high command. In fact, according to German statistics, about three million horses and mules saw service during the war years between 1939 and 1945.

The translated and edited German manual, Tentative Instructions for the Training and Tactics of Ski Troops, *special series #20, published in 1944 by the U.S. War Department, describes the differences in training between the veteran German mountain soldiers and the fledgling American 10th Mountain Division.*

Ski troops are the most mobile arm of the infantry in mountainous areas and snow-covered terrain. Because of their special training and equipment, these units can execute combat missions lasting several days without support from other forces.

The aim of this training is to achieve skiing proficiency as well as a high standard of military training in general. Development of endurance and an effortless cross-country style will be stressed. Instruction in pulling hand sleds and preparing tracks will also be covered.

The success of any ski unit depends primarily on its mobility and speed. The training of the ordinary soldier—and all subordinate leaders—must be guided by that principle. The condition of skis and sled equipment is equally important.

Officers and enlisted men possessing special proficiency—or experience in winter warfare—will be placed on detached service and shall become instructors regardless of rank.

Strenuous marches, including night bivouacs, will be included in the training schedule. During these exercises, peacetime comforts will not be permitted.

Company and platoon commanders will lead their men in all kinds of weather and must be proficient in every weapon at their disposal. Officers of all ranks must possess excellent agility, hardiness, willingness to accept responsibility, and, most of all, initiative. They must also share the physical hardships and privations with the men under their command. In every situation, advantage will be taken of favorable climatic conditions. The enemy should always be confronted whenever he is the most fatigued—and our men are well rested.

If possible, combat positions should be established in terrain that is unfavorable for a counterattack but that permits our troops to shift locations or withdraw under cover. Because of their limited ammunition supply, ski units are not suited for prolonged engagements.

The best time for carrying out harassing missions is at night. The attack should be made from a direction that will facilitate the cutting of enemy communications. If a mission is only partially successful, the unit commander will decide whether or not to abandon it.

In snow-covered terrain, enemy infantry, without skis, can be hit hard against its flanks. At the same time, a bold frontal attack might also be successful. This kind of enveloping action—utilizing the mobility afforded by skis—is the most effective type of onslaught.

Envelopment of enemy positions should be executed with simultaneous reconnaissance to the front and flanks. This will enable the attacking force to bypass strong emplacements and to completely encircle the opposing troops.

The encirclement can be tightened by means of small harassing units striking from various directions. At the same time, a few squads, armed with machine guns, can be assigned to defend against any counterattacks.

The assembling of an attack force should be shrouded as much as possible and expedited by secretly cutting trails in advance. The infantry is always the last unit to move into an assembly area. The time interval between preparation and the actual attack must be kept to a minimum, since lying in the snow and cold is debilitating.

If it is impossible for a ski unit to reach the assembly area without being observed; it may be advisable to try to deceive the enemy by having men trickle into the location singly, or in groups, and at irregular intervals. This method, however, requires considerably more time and will be used only if weather permits a long stay.

At the beginning of any operation, heavy infantry weapons and artillery pieces will be positioned forward in order for them to support the attacking force as long as possible. But rapid changes of location can be facilitated by preparing tracks in advance. It should be remembered, however, that the emplacement of heavy weapons takes at least twice as long in snow and severe cold as it does under normal conditions.

The superiority of a well-trained, swift-moving ski unit is most effective in the pursuit of the enemy. A flanking chase—across unguarded, pathless terrain—combined with a frontal assault is the most effective combat strategy.

During the pursuit, an effort must always be made to cut the enemy off from his line of retreat. At the same time, an enveloping maneuver on both flanks can try to force him into a small pocket. However, to increase mobility, some equipment, heavy weapons, and sleds must usually be left behind.

The ski troops will pursue the withdrawing enemy day and night, and use ambushes to continually harass his retreating forces.

A ski unit's defensive capabilities are always evident in its mobility. The backbone of any defense consists of strong points established far to the front and suitable for all-around protection. Heavy weapons, with ample supplies of ammunition, should be brought to these locations as soon as possible.

A no-man's-land area must be continually reconnoitered by ski patrols and suitable sites safeguarded by protective trails. Dummy installations—which can be quickly set up in snowy terrain—will be employed in large numbers. And camouflage must be used to hide the construction of shelters and campgrounds.

Reserve troops will stay under cover in shelters or dugouts so that when called upon, they can go into combat rested and warm. Our counterattacks, should be directed against the flanks of a charging enemy—who must be annihilated with concentrated fire at point-blank range and in hand-to-hand fighting. The most effective action in this case is a pincer movement, executed by several assault columns, for the purpose of encircling and destroying the enemy force.

Assault-gun units are excellent for supporting ski troops. The employment of this kind of weaponry during winter is dependent on terrain and snow conditions. Engineers must also be assigned to clear roads and remove mines. And, because of the difficulty of target recognition on a field of bright snow, range-finding is most important.

The use of ski troops is flexible but requires exact cooperation with our air force. All members of a ski unit must be familiar with the use of identification signals and codes between ground and air elements. If and when a ski patrol penetrates deep behind enemy lines, it must mark its boundries by flags, panels, or smoke signals.

Long-range missions may necessitate ski units being supplied by air. In this case, the drop sites should be located in an open area—but far enough from the front lines to be safe from enemy observation.

Ski troops can give considerable support to foot soldiers because, by not using regular roads or trails, ski troops are able to move rapidly to where they are needed the most. In this regard, they can also be employed as an enveloping force or in pursuit and rear-guard actions.

Surprise and deception are very important. These factors are usually made possible by long winter nights, poor visibility, and the superior mobility of ski troops in almost any kind of weather.

Because it is very arduous for ski soldiers to bring artillery with them, they must usually accomplish their mission without heavy gun support. Therefore, in order to gain fire superiority, it is necessary to concentrate the assault at the main point of attack.

A ski unit, whose mission may lead it into unknown territory, is in great danger of being surprised by the enemy. Unceasing reconnaissance, extra security, and an ever-alert eye are prime requisites for all operations. Fatigue of the troops will not be used as an excuse for the neglect of necessary measures for security.

Reconnaissance should be made on a broad front and in such a manner that the enemy cannot draw any conclusions as to the direction of an attack. Intelligence concerning the enemy's winter road network is essential in determining not only the line of our assault but also the direction of a possible counterattack.

The use of a raiding party is chiefly to destroy distant objectives and for quick sorties behind enemy lines. These units must be able to accomplish their missions independently while fighting on an original ration of supplies and ammunition. Raiders can be effective in destroying enemy artillery positions, command posts, supply and ammunition facilities, and communication lines.

The guiding factors in selecting personnel for these ski groups are aggressiveness, skiing proficiency, and marksmanship. Men who speak the enemy's language are particularly advantageous.

In training the individual rifleman, various firing positions will be practiced with and without skis. Soldiers who qualify as sharpshooters will be issued rifles equipped with telescopic sights.

Each man must also learn to use the light machine gun and the submachine gun. In addition, a knowledge of the enemy's weaponry is desirable.

The typical ski patrol consists of one squad. For certain missions, however, it can be reinforced with engineers, artillery observers, and a radio team.

The strength of an attacking force can range from a platoon to a company. As a rule, heavy armament—including antitank weapons—are included. However, the mobility of the unit must not be impaired. Certain weapons, loaded on hand sleds, are preferable to those that must be moved only on horse-drawn sleds.

The equipment carried by the ski soldiers must be of the lightest possible weight and based on the tactical requirements of the operation. Written orders—including maps with overlays—must not be taken along.

Maximum firepower and mobility are the decisive factors in determining the type and number of weapons issued to each man. If a choice must be made between the amount of ammunition and the number of weapons, less arms and more ammunition should be the rule.

Prepared foods, rich in fat, that does not occupy much space and is not affected by weather, will be the rations for ski troops. Every third man will carry cooking implements.

Bivouac items will be taken along in case the troops must camp in the snow and cold. Although the tents that retain heat are heavier, they are preferable to those that do not.

There should be at least two compasses for each squad, plus binoculars and watches. A number of arrows, flags, paint, and colored paper should be carried for marking trails.

Medical equipment will be carried on a hand sled and will consist mainly of bandages, wire-ladder splints, antifrost ointment, and stimulants. Sleds will also be used to transport the wounded.

It is indispensable for even the smallest unit to have ski-repair equipment—including parts for bindings and spare tips for skis. For long missions, spare skis and poles should be carried.

The prime requisites for all patrols and raiding parties are courage and a ruthless, aggressive spirit. Quick action—utilizing the element of surprise—can gain superiority, even against a far stronger enemy.

Certain procedures should be followed for a successful surprise attack. Ski patrols should be mobile—get off the roads—and approach the enemy cross-country through wooded areas. It is also advisable to utilize the darkness of night and foggy weather to penetrate the enemy positions.

If a ski unit is ordered to go on a mission behind enemy lines, it first must determine if there are gaps in the enemy's front and if the flanks can be bypassed.

It is very important that our troops should avoid numerically superior and equally mobile enemy units—especially if the mission can be accomplished without a combat situation developing. An envelopment, or surprise attack by the enemy, must be prevented by increased watchfulness.

The strategy for every mission must be made known to each member of the ski patrol or raiding party. The plan should cover the route of march, the plan of action for contact with the enemy, execution of the assignment, and the rendezvous point after completion of the mission. The return route will be indicated during the approach march and marked where necessary.

The best time to attempt a mission behind enemy lines is during the early hours of evening, when the ski unit can use the darkness to penetrate far into the enemy's rear without being detected.

During daylight hours, the troops will bivouac in remote and concealed areas. In extended missions, the bivouacs are suitable as departure points for continuing operations and can also be converted into supply dumps.

Because of their mobility, ski troops are able to speedily locate the enemy—who is usually operating in trackless terrain—and to annihilate him by systematically prepared surprise attacks.

Above all, the objective of these attacks must be the raiding and destruction of hostile operating bases. Actions against enemy units are most effective when they are cut off from their main group and are exposed to the bitter cold and the difficulties of supply.

During winter weather, ski and sled tracks can give away the enemy's position and, even at great distances, can disclose information about his strength and disposition of forces. It must be borne in mind, however, that a tough and shrewd enemy may also be prowling behind our lines.

The usual formation for an approach is single file. In order to shorten the distance between the ski soldiers—which is about five times that of foot soldiers—our troops should advance in several parallel columns. Units with horse-drawn sleds will proceed close together in a single line.

For short distances, a firm path for sleds can be made by packing the snow. This can be done very effectively by a snowshoe detail.

In order to save energy, uphill tracks should have as few turns as possible. Slopes should be uniform and adapted to the most inexperienced skier. When approaching a curve, skis are not to be raised off the ground. They must slide along the snow to the desired direction. If ski tracks are too narrow, they become useless. An eight-inch width is suitable for most skiers.

Heavy snowfalls can obliterate tracks in a short time. It then becomes necessary to send a trail-breaking detachment ahead in advance of the main unit.

The distance covered by the trailbreakers depends on the terrain and the type of snow. To maintain endurance and guarantee an uninterrupted advance, the lead men of the detachment should be relieved often. In heavy snow, this may be ordered about every three hundred feet. Members of a well-trained unit usually relieve each other without specific orders.

Every trail-breaking detachment should mark its path as uniformly as possible. The type of markings used should be simple and familiar to the troops—and should be recognizable at night as well as day. Unobtrusive markers are sufficient for temporary trails. Paths intended for frequent use, however, should be permanently marked. In order to prevent the detection of fresh trails, they must be made along the contours of the natural terrain—such as gorges, knolls, ditches, and woods.

The difference between success and failure of any mission is often dependent on camouflage. Snow completely changes a landscape and conceals details of the terrain from enemy ground and air observation. On the other hand, however, troop and vehicle trails are easily discernable.

When maneuvering in snow, ski soldiers should wear white cloaks and two-piece white uniforms. In addition, the men should wear white gloves and cover their faces with gauze masks.

There are times when it may become necessary to improvise camouflage. If the steel helmet is not painted white, it can be pasted over with white paper. The paper should reach down to the shoulders and cover the face. Slits can be made for the eyes.

However, the easiest way to camouflage the head and shoulders is to fasten one end of a white towel to the helmet and pin the other end to the shoulders. The face is then covered by a white handkerchief, which is drawn back and pinned to the towel.

Cloaks can be made from white sheets. Remnants of old colored garments should be sewed on one side as a lining, so that the multicolored half of the cape can be worn in a nonsnow landscape.

Horses can be camouflaged using white blankets without interfering with their vision and breathing. The most effective camouflage for weapons, equipment, vehicles, and sleds is white oil paint or whitewash. If they are not available, chalk or lime dissolved in water will serve the purpose.

A soldier, completely clothed in white, is able to move about freely in snow-covered terrain. Even in good weather, he can hardly be seen from a distance of a few hundred yards. And, when lying prone, he can remain invisible to the enemy at a much closer range.

When moving, however, the ski trooper must constantly utilize a white background and select his position accordingly. And, upon exiting a wooded area, he must creep through the snow until he is beyond the shadow of the tree line.

Winter conditions often make it difficult to distinguish between friend and foe—even at short distances. Therefore, the use of certain distinctive identification markers are necessary. Black or red armbands, three inches wide, should be worn on the sleeve. To avoid imitation by the enemy, they can be changed periodically—just like passwords.

It is also important to know the use of colored pennants for communication purposes between land and air units. Special prearranged signals between air and ground forces have proved very effective. In improvising flags, only dark conspicuous colors should be used.

Various markings in the snow—such as three close impressions made with the ring of a ski pole—could be a sign. Also, broken twigs on trees can be used as predetermined signals.

Falling snow and fog can necessitate frequent trail-marking. Orientation is facilitated if the markers are numbered successively in the direction of the march and spaced at uniform intervals. In order to avoid damage to the signs, they should be placed about three feet off the path. Any strange tracks crossing the trail must be obliterated. It may also be advisable to post sentries at crossings to direct units that are to follow.

Snowmen have proved invaluable as markers. They should be approximately four feet high with a small opening about thirty inches above the ground. A pane of ice is set in the cavity and will reflect rays of light that can be seen over long distances—even when visibility is poor.

For recognition purposes in fog or darkness, a colored blinker system using flashlights is very effective. However, the sequence of colors must be prearranged—such as a red signal answered by a green one.

Packed snow, along with cold weather, carry any sound through the chilled air. Therefore, any unnecessary noise must be avoided. During a stealthy advance, certain members of each column should be detailed to frequently stop and listen for sounds of enemy activity.

Flank and rear guards must be as mobile as possible and equipped with the absolute minimum of hand sleds. When visibility is good, these soldiers can move rapidly from one observation point to another.

On the approach of enemy aircraft, the ski troops must disperse and take cover by crouching over their skis. Any skis that are not painted white should be immediately covered with snow. The men must remain motionless in this position until the all-clear is signaled. Horse-drawn sleds will remain on the pathway, and drivers will stay with the animals.

All riflemen and machine gun crews will defend against low-flying hostile planes. In order to try to deceive enemy air observers, it is advisable to have a special squad whose job it is to cover the tracks left behind by the advancing soldiers. This precaution is most important when leaving bivouacs and wooded areas.

Leaders of all grades must strive to maintain the continuity of the march—even under adverse climatic conditions. The pace of the advance must not be allowed to slacken, even on slight uphill slopes, and troops should not bunch up at the start or finish of a downhill stretch.

Obstacles should be negotiated on the broadest possible front without slowing the march. Rear units must be warned of dangers ahead.

This can be accomplished by erecting signs, using word of mouth, or posting sentries.

One officer should be detailed to supervise march discipline. If a man falls out of the column, he must step aside, clear the path, and report his trouble to the last man in line.

After advancing for forty-five minutes, a short fifteen-minute rest should be ordered for tightening ski bindings and checking hand sleds. During this halt, skis must not be removed, and sleds should stay on the trail. However, the frequency of rest periods depends on the situation—including cold, snow, suitable stopping places, and the degree of fatigue exhibited by the troops.

During periods of extreme cold and sharp winds, a major effort should be made to accomplish the march without stopping. In this kind of weather, rest periods do no good and can easily cause colds and other illnesses. Wooded areas, underbrush, and ravines make the most suitable rest sites and offer concealment from ground and air observation.

Ski troops should not be deprived of their freedom of action, no matter how inclement the weather. They must try every possible way to attack the enemy and destroy him. Mobility and the capacity to deceive and outwit a foe can give even a weaker force a sense of superiority.

When stopping after a long march and skis are removed, they must be placed on the snow with running surfaces down. In case of a thaw, however, they should be planted in the snow with tips down. During long stops, skis should be rewaxed.

If time permits, wet underclothing should be changed and warm drinks issued. Snow should not be used to quench thirst. All tracks made during a rest period must be erased when the advance is resumed. The march should then begin at a moderate pace—gradually accelerating to the normal speed.

Tracks of unknown origin sighted in the snow must be treated with suspicion. They may have been purposely made by the enemy for an ambush or even mined.

Ski troop detachments can prevent the enemy from learning an accurate estimate of their strength by having each man insert his ski pole in the same hole as the soldier ahead of him—or by keeping ski poles raised for a specified period of time. Consequently, the enemy will be unable to estimate the number of men he is facing—even if he counts the pole marks in the snow.

Engineers should be placed at the front of the column and adequately equipped to remove obstacles. Bringing up the rear of the line should be hand sleds carrying extra skis, spare parts, and repair tools.

The approach to the enemy's position should be accomplished by quick movements—from one surveillance point to another. If it is necessary to cross open areas that are subject to observation—especially during day-light—a detachment should be deployed to provide protection until the entire section has passed the danger zone.

At night, silent movements are essential. In case of moonlight, the march should follow a shadowed route. Wind direction may also be an important factor in selecting the direction of an approach.

When within range of the enemy, a quick decision must be made as to whether skis should be stacked and snowshoes put on—and exactly where the hand sleds should be positioned. If it becomes necessary to use detours or terrain unfavorable for skiing, the men will advance on foot.

At all times, our troops must attempt to gain the heights from where they can make a rapid descent across an area that is under enemy fire or observation.

Combat and tactical measures depend on the mission. Reconnaissance ski patrols should avoid contact with the enemy unless they have no choice. Assault units and raiding parties, however, require bold actions, the aim of which is to give the enemy no rest and to weaken and paralyze his ability to fight.

At night, in wooded areas, a small ski detachment can shake the morale of the enemy with mobile and surprise attacks. Careful preparation and lightning strikes are the basis for success in missions of this kind.

The location and strength of the enemy as well as the terrain must be adequately reconnoitered before entering battle. But, extreme care should be taken that the enemy has not guessed where and when the attack will take place.

Any action must always be opened by surprise fire. The quicker and harder the foe is hit, the less likely he will be able to take effective defensive measures. In order to deceive the enemy, it may be necessary to stage the attack on a broad front or else have several different units open fire simultaneously from different directions.

Unrelenting attacks are the proven method for winter warfare. They deprive the enemy of any rest, throttle his supply lines, and force him to make frequent counterattacks. Thus, his fighting strength is sapped without appreciably weakening our forces.

Breaking through enemy lines is difficult and costly—especially on unfamiliar terrain. Therefore, it is advantageous to isolate him by cutting communication lines. This will force the enemy soldiers to move out of their warm shelters and into the cold.

Disengaging from a battle is an essential part of any mission and must be provided for in every operational plan. At times, a withdrawal might prove more difficult than the approach. The method will depend on the situation and the terrain. In an orderly retreat, the commanding officer will designate the men and weapons that are to remain in contact with the enemy. If possible, the main unit will retire on a previously marked track.

The mobility of ski troops makes a withdrawal from action more rapid than regular infantry and can often be effectively carried out in daylight. This is especially true if the retreat can be accomplished by a downhill run.

As a rule, heavy weapons loaded on sleds are the first to leave the area in case of a retirement. And, if the situation permits, they can be used from a rear position to cover the withdrawal of our forces.

Ski trails can remain visible for long periods of time and could betray the path of retreat. It is imperative to deceive the enemy as to the return route. This can be accomplished by making dummy tracks and posting false signs.

In fresh-fallen snow, trails can be blurred by tree branches or barbed wire dragged along by the last man in the column. If the enemy is in close pursuit, as many delays as possible must be put in his way. These can include ambushes, roadblocks, and the mining of trails.

Organizing for defense on frozen ground requires much time and labor. Experience has shown that the main zone of resistance must be held as an uninterrupted line—particularly at night—in order to prevent infiltration by the enemy. It is also necessary to establish several strong points to protect against surprise attacks. An enemy force that has broken through our defenses must be repulsed before it can gain a foothold.

Every commanding officer must always be aware of the fact that he has the responsibility of keeping his men healthy. Food rations are a top priority. Hot soups should be served frequently with breakfast and supper. Alcoholic drinks should be issued only at night and in bivouac. Rum should not be given out unless it is mixed with hot coffee or tea. If cognac or vodka is distributed, care must be taken that any soldier does not receive more than his share—either as a gift or by trading.

Whenever field kitchens cannot be set up, powdered coffee, tea, and other foods will be distributed so that the soldiers can prepare their own meals. However, only essential rations will be issued—otherwise, the men will throw away whatever seems superfluous at the moment. Flour rations can be stretched by adding sawdust—preferably from pine trees, but birch bark can also be used.

During cold weather and snow, special measures must be taken to transport food. Commissary wagons should be built with double walls packed with hay or wood shavings, and the floors should be covered with straw. Food containers must be protected with straw mats and blankets.

Because of a shortage of ski boots, laced shoes can be adapted by attaching a metal strip from a tin can to the sole of the shoe and then bending it upward on each side of the toe. This will protect the shoe and permit it to sit better in the ski binding. The metal strip should be fastened to the sole by small nails.

Felt boots and overshoes can be worn over laced shoes. But the overshoes are only issued in three sizes. If the overshoe is too large, the empty space can be stuffed with paper, straw, rags, or dry moss.

If there is a shortage of skis and sleds, they can be confiscated from the civilian population. Sleds can also be fabricated by the ski troops, but the width of the runners must be standardized.

The speedy transfer of wounded to dressing stations is imperative. The difficult conditions of winter warfare necessitate special measures for recovering the injured, and the best skiers must be used for this purpose.

A comparatively fast and safe means of moving the wounded can be had by using shelter halves or hand sleds. Horses, if needed, should always be available to pull the sleds.

Evacuation routes should correspond with supply trails and be marked with signposts. A number of horse-drawn sleds that haul supplies to the front can carry wounded soldiers on their return trip.

All sleds used as ambulances should have a bed of loose straw or fir twigs as protection against the cold and jolting. The sleds should be equipped with warming bottles, chemical warming bags, or sacks filled with hot sand. Care must be taken, however, that the wounded men are not burned—especially if they are unconscious or shell-shocked. It is also important that the sleds be supplied with canteens of hot drinks, which can be kept warm in buckets of hot sand.

CHAPTER 3

The 87th Mountain Infantry Regiment: The Kiska Campaign

In his memoirs, Walter E. Howard described ski training at Camp Hale and the invasion of Kiska.

Skiing in the Rocky Mountains was great fun, except for the fact that we had to carry large, heavy backpacks. Night skiing was the most hazardous. If there were no fires or camp lights to create shadows, a skier could blindly crash into a vertical snowbank—and with serious consequences.

On one weekend ski trip, a buddy and I were moving along a ridge when a strong wind blew us off the ledge. To survive the night, we dug horizontal tunnels in the snow. The next day, however, it was impossible to climb up to the ridge, so we had a long ski trip back to camp. Luckily, most of it was downhill.

Another weekend, I was one of eight men who were sent out to scale the face of Holy Cross Mountain. We were to test winter climbing equipment. Late in the day, our leader—an experienced mountaineer—began to suffer altitude sickness. I thought he would soon recover, so I gave the others both our packs and said I would stay with him until he was able to resume the climb.

The others continued on to a stone shelter farther up the slope. They tried to communicate with us by shouts, but the distance was too great to understand any words.

The sick soldier did not recover, forcing the two of us to remain all night on the exposed and dangerous side of the mountain. I finally gave up trying to answer the shouts of the men above me. They now assumed we had probably slipped and fallen—and pondered how to go about finding our bodies six thousand feet below.

In the meantime, I kept probing the rock with my ski pole. I finally found a large snow-filled crevice and quickly dug out a narrow trench large enough for both of us. We had no sooner squeezed into the opening—and covered the trench with our skis—than blowing snow swiftly sealed us in.

Fortunately, we did not suffer from the below-zero temperature outside. The next morning, we headed back down the mountain and were happily met by a truck.

Our basic ski training at Camp Hale was exciting but also very frustrating. Many of the officers and enlisted men were not true mountaineers. And, because there was no training manual for mountain troops, we had to use infantry manuals. Therefore, many foolish mistakes were made that could be life-threatening in actual combat. Morale among the ski troopers began to decline. I had my parents ship me my late brother's musical instruments in hopes they would lift the morale in my company.

One night while on maneuvers—and using a candle in my sleeping bag—I wrote a list of suggested improvements on how troops should operate in the snow. After returning to camp, I handed the brilliant recommendations to my first sergeant, who probably had the lowest IQ in the company. My reward? I was immediately assigned to KP duty and vociferously informed that privates were to follow orders, not make suggestions. I am positive that he destroyed the only copy of my late-night labors.

After practicing amphibious landings with Higgins boats along the California coast, we boarded a troop transport and steamed into San Diego Harbor for a day of recreation before sailing to Kiska.

As soon as the first group of ski troops returned to the ship after a few hours of liberty, the second section prepared to go ashore. But then, for some unexplained reason, the ship's captain announced over the bullhorn that all shore leave was canceled. We were not told the reason for this directive, and since ski troopers were the think-for-yourself outdoors type—who always expected to know "why" when strange orders were given—this announcement almost caused a riot.

One of my friends stripped down to his shorts, put his clothes in a plastic bag, and threw the sack into the water. He then jumped overboard, retrieved his clothes, and began swimming toward shore. Despite our shouts of encouragement, his freedom was short-lived. The ship's launch was quickly lowered and captured my buddy, and he was thrown in the brig.

This insult—our hero in the ship's jail—was more than the ski troops could take. We immediately organized and threatened to throw every sailor over the side unless our comrade was released. After a period of intense negotiations, our officers managed to convince the transport's commanding officer that the ski troops would probably carry out the mutinous threats. The soldier was released without punishment, and a tense calm pervaded the ship.

It was not long, however, before another edict almost caused a revolution. While training for winter warfare at Camp Hale, we always used rucksacks to carry our ammunition and gear. But, the day before leaving for Kiska, the army's commanding officer learned of a regulation stating that when making amphibious landings, the troops must wear the old-style army haversack instead of our more modern rucksacks. Then, from somewhere in the bowels of the troopship, officers located a supply of haversacks and proceeded to issue them to the ski troopers. None of us had ever worn a haversack, and we were not about to give up our familiar rucksacks. We promptly threw the haversacks overboard, and that settled the issue.

A short time later, however, the commander had another bright idea. Apparently, he decided that we did not have enough firepower and began issuing some of us unfamiliar automatic weapons. But there was no way any of the ski troopers would accept a weapon they had never fired, and we threatened to toss the guns into the sea. After a spirited discussion, we were allowed to keep our original weapons, which we could clean and assemble blindfolded.

Upon our arrival at Kiska, the navy began bombarding the island and making fake landings at Kiska Harbor. Our transport anchored on the other side of the island. The ski troopers climbed down cargo nets to the waiting landing craft. The Higgins boats plowed through the icy surf toward shore.

We landed on a rock-strewn beach, and many of the men became thoroughly soaked when they slipped on the slimy stones. We immediately began to climb a precipitous mountain.

The ski troops were nervous and tense the night before the invasion, and sleep was difficult. Every fifth or seventh round of our ammunition was a tracer shell, and we began shooting at every suspicious shadow or movement. Whenever a tracer ricocheted off a rock, you could swear that the enemy was firing back at us. All the bullets whizzing about soon gave the impression that the Japanese were dug in along the face of the mountain.

The swirling fog, whipped by strong winds, made it difficult to see, or even hear, friendly challenges. The passwords were "long limb" and "that thing." These words were thought to be difficult for the Japanese to pronounce.

As the ski troops moved forward, we came upon abandoned enemy machine guns. At first we assumed that the Japanese had withdrawn farther up the slope. (We later learned that all the guns were missing their firing mechanism.)

When we arrived at the summit, it was almost humorous how everyone outdid badgers in the speed at which we dug foxholes.

Emotional strain can affect the nerves of battle-green men and their leaders. Our first sergeant was so afraid of his own men that he had the bugler share his foxhole.

We had no sooner dug in than Colonel Henderson began sending out radio messages stating that the enemy was infiltrating—first from one direction, then from all directions. These frantic calls had an anxious effect on the jittery ski troops and were taken to mean that if you saw someone moving in the thick fog, you had better shoot him before he shot you.

The colonel's nervous voice became more excitable. He asked for a number of men from my unit (Company I) to come down and protect the battalion headquarters against attack. Lieutenant Wilfred Funk assembled some troops to comply with the order. As he and his men carefully groped their way through the heavy mist—trying to find a safe path downhill—they suddenly stumbled upon a group of dug-in ski troopers. Because of the fog—and the bedlam of noise caused by a naval shelling of Kiska Harbor—it was impossible to hear passwords. Each group assumed that the other was enemy. Funk's men began throwing grenades, and the ski troops opened fire with machine guns. When the smoke cleared, two officers and nine men had been killed, and eleven others wounded, by friendly fire.

Meanwhile, the rest of Company I remained dug in on the ridge and still had not made contact with the enemy. It became obvious that a squad should be sent out to locate the Japanese before they zeroed in on us. Our officers were unwilling to lead a patrol, so a small group of us took over the mission. My squad corporal insisted that I should not be on the point since I was the only married man on the patrol.

It's amazing how nervous anxiety will affect a man after he has gone about seventy-two hours without sleep. As we moved cautiously through the foggy mist, one member of our party fired his rifle and said that he shot a Japanese soldier. We searched the area, but there was no sign of a body. Ten minutes later, he opened fire again and claimed that he shot another one of the enemy. However, once again, the body was not found.

I had noticed previously that Japanese canteens we had come across were shaped differently from the American type. I asked the soldier to describe the second man he shot, which he did in great detail. But, when I asked him to describe the enemy canteen, it was the same kind that we carried. I immediately realized what was happening and convinced him that the Japanese soldiers were figments of his imagination. The fog and lack of sleep contributed to the optical illusions.

The day after we learned that the enemy had apparently escaped from the island, our emotional response was to act foolishly. We began exploring the many crawl-size caves that the Japanese had dug, but only after defusing any booby traps in our way.

We found one large cache of enemy ammunition. It had been hidden under netting and covered with vegetation. We built a fire nearby and took turns throwing packages of the ammunition into the flames. The fireworks were really exciting. After each explosion, we would measure to see who had lain down closest to the detonation. This dangerous game ended when one of the explosions was so heavy that all of us shed a little blood. Fortunately, we were able to patch ourselves up.

Our next stupid stunt was to climb down the steep back side of the mountain and sit on a vertical rocky bluff about ten feet above the ocean. From this precarious position, we took turns dropping grenades into the water. The object of the game was to see whose grenade would go off underwater but closest to the surface. We knew that if one of them exploded in midair, we would all be killed. Fortunately, the contest was called off before that happened.

Demolition troops were soon sent in to clean up the ammunition dumps, and several of us were assigned to help with the task. After an hour or so, it suddenly dawned on me that these explosive experts had been trained for this type of work, but were using us to defuse booby traps instead of risking their own lives. We accused the captain in charge of the demolition crew of unscrupulous conduct and then returned to our company. The captain was embarrassed, but he did not try pull rank and stop us from leaving.

One thing we could do nothing about was the weather. Periodically, cyclic storms formed in the Bering Sea. One day we would have hurricane-force winds from one direction—followed by a dead calm—then hurricane-force winds from the opposite direction. When the wind was very strong, you could hold out a cup of coffee and the cup would be immediately drained.

Because of the gale-force winds, it was impossible to urinate without having the fluid spray back in your face. Finally, one brilliant soldier discovered that mortar shell casings made a perfect windproof urinal. It did not take long before the area was littered with discarded mortar casings.

Because of the perpetual fog and dampness, everything was always wet. At night, while on the ridge, we slept in shelves that we carved out on the sides of the foxholes. Every night before crawling into our wet sleeping bags, we would have a buddy take one end of the bag. Then we would wring as much water as possible out of it, give it a few shakes, and crawl in. No wonder I suffered for years from rheumatism in one shoulder.

One morning when we were falling out for the day's work assignments, the fog suddenly lifted and we had our first view of the impressive Kiska volcano. I whispered to my friend, Henry Moscow, "Pass the word, if I don't appear for tomorrow morning's formation." No other words were necessary. Henry understood my fake sick call. He knew that I just had to climb that volcano. He would have gone with me, but we both realized that the climb would be too strenuous for him. It had to be a solo mission. There was no time to recruit someone else, and it would be difficult for more than one person to sneak away.

It was a rough ascent, but I finally reached the summit of the volcano. The wind was so strong at the top that at ten feet or so from the rim, I was forced to crawl on my stomach.

There was a fissure on the north side of the volcano wall. Whenever clouds rushed through the opening—then out a nearby crevice—different pitches of sound could be heard, depending on the size of the cloud.

I could not see the bottom of the crater because of the smoke, but the odor of sulfur was very strong. I slid backwards over the edge and carefully moved down the verticle wall. The wind was so fierce that for the first few feet, I was almost suspended in air.

Upon reaching the floor of the crater, I noticed several sulfur fumaroles, each a yard or so in diameter. I padded my ears for protection from the deafening roar then crawled closer, where I was treated to a remarkable view of the beautiful colors boiling up from the vents. On the upwind side of the fumaroles, the pure sulfur was about ten feet deep. I collected some samples to take back to camp.

While scouting the volcano, I came across the wreckage of a crashed aircraft. Two people had been buried under the rocks. I salvaged pieces of aluminum from the plane and later made bracelets etched with the ski troop insignia. The soldiers were eager to buy them.

By the time I returned to camp after the long, arduous hike, my blisters had blisters. It was a trip that could not have been made in the short time available with another person along.

While we were still on Kiska, a new colonel arrived to take over command. He planned an exercise to show how he would have carried out the invasion. Before beginning the march, each man was issued two chocolate bars. At some point during the maneuver, there was to be an inspection to make sure that none of us had prematurely eaten the candy. I think I devoured the first bar before I was handed the second.

It was not long before the colonel had another bright idea. He asked me to lead a detachment up the volcano. I ducked out when he kept insisting that the men carry their weapons during the climb. I knew this was too dangerous and that I would be the fall guy if any accidents happened. The end result was that the troops did not carry weapons, and I missed out on a second ascent.

One day while serving on guard duty, I was reprimanded by the colonel for not standing and saluting him. He declared that if we were in combat, he could shoot me. I answered that if we were in combat he would make a perfect target if an enemy sniper observed the salute.

That night, two of my buddies strolled near his tent. One of them commented, loud enough for the colonel to hear, "Have you still got your round for the colonel?" The other soldier replied, "Yes!" It was not long after that the colonel was transferred off the island.

The Kiska campaign cost the lives of twenty-nine ski troopers, and fifty-five others were wounded. After things calmed down, every officer and noncom in my company took a trip to the hospital ship for treatment of jittery nerves.

While the ski troopers marked time before leaving Kiska, some wit worked up a song to the tune of the barroom ballad, "No Balls at All":

> We headed for Kiska with blood in our eye,
> But G-2 had told us a hell of a lie!
> Ten thousand Jap soldiers were due for a fall—
> But when we arrived, there were no Japs at all!
>
> *Chorus*
> What? No Japs at all! Yes, no Japs at all!
> A very small island with no Japs at all!
> We learned how to ski, and we learned how to climb,
> We learned how to stay out in any ol' clime,
> We jumped on our skis when they gave us the call—
> Then came to an island with no Japs at all!

Another song followed the tune of the navy's "Bell Bottom Trousers." It was the story of a barmaid in a mountain inn seduced by a skier off the slopes:

> Now if you have a daughter bounce her on your knee,
> And if you have a son send the bastard out to ski!
>
> *Chorus*
> Singing ninety pounds rucksack, a pound of grub or two,
> He'll schuss the mountain like his daddy used to do!

John E. Fitzgerald's story of the Aleutian campaign is edited from his self-published booklet, Memoirs of a Ski-Trooper, 1942–1945.

We arrived off Kiska Island on August 14, 1943. Our landing was set for the following morning. Throughout the day, many orders were issued along with inspections of equipment and packs. It seemed as though our rucksacks were inspected hourly to make sure they were packed correctly. The list of items was strictly enforced (dry socks, clean underwear, etc.). There was a certain required article, however, that none of us could understand—one new mattress cover. I thought to myself, "What the hell is this for? There's not a mattress within five hundred miles of here!" The Graves Registration officer supplied the gruesome answer. We were to carry our own shrouds!

There were a few funny moments aboard ship, especially when camouflage makeup was issued—green and black grease paint, jungle colors. After all, this was the Pacific. (In 1945, when I was receiving my disability discharge, a doctor on the board questioned my discharge because I had been in the Pacific theater and had never received my yellow fever shots!)

About noon on the 14th, we all assembled in the main dining room to hear a long telegram from FDR wishing us Godspeed. Then, later in the day, we had a gigantic feast—broiled steak, french fries, and all the fixings. For dessert, the cooks brought out a monstrous cake baked in the shape of Kiska Island. Somewhere during all the festivities, the chaplain gave a long benediction—one of the best morale ruiners ever invented.

Sleep was out of the question that night. I was assigned to the lead Higgins boat. We climbed aboard about 2 A.M. with full packs, inflated Mae Wests, and rifles. Positioned on the boat's deck were many canisters of 81mm mortar shells. Upon hitting the beach, we were to carry a mortar shell in each hand and stack them for the weapons platoon.

Also on the landing craft was a large thermos of hot tea, supposedly laced with medicinal brandy. It probably only contained a small amount of alcohol, but it was enough to cause frequent urges to urinate. But where? Then someone came up with a brilliant suggestion—remove the shells from the canisters and use the cans as urinals. This plan did not go over well with some of the men who asked, "Wouldn't live mortar shells, rolling across the pitching deck, be dangerous?" The answer, "You bet! Throw the fuckers overboard!"

It was about dawn when we began our approach to the beach. Ted Miller, the assistant cook, organized a prayer meeting in one corner of the boat. Private John Wolff—the company alcoholic—was standing alone gazing out at the rolling sea. He was asked if he would like to join the group. "Hell no," he replied. "It's too late now!"

Guarding our run to shore were two World War I antique coal-burning destroyers with tall stacks shooting out thick clouds of black smoke and sooty sparks. The U.S. Navy sure wasn't going to gamble any worthwhile vessels on this risky venture.

The Coast Guard coxswain of our boat—who was getting three times his daily pay for hazardous duty—dropped the ramp. As we climbed over the rocks, the coxswain slammed the ramp shut, threw the engine into reverse, and scurried back to the ship—scared shitless.

I have forgotten much of that long first day on the island, probably because nothing happened until dark. We spread out over the slippery tundra and climbed a hill. Every now and then I heard a rifle shot. We reached our objective before dark and were told to dig foxholes. At our sector a man needed dynamite to dig a hole in the rocky ground. The best I could do was to hack and scrape a spot level enough to sleep on without rolling down the slope. All this time, there was the shifting wind (called a williwaw), hard and soft rain, and a dense or wispy fog.

The night was a nightmare with little or no rest. Shots were fired off and on. Someone nearby fired a string of bullets from a tommy gun. I never remembered hearing a Jap rifle. But I knew it was a .07 caliber, which would not sound as loud as our Mls—and certainly could not equal the noise made by the .45-caliber tommy guns.

At daylight, the medics began recovering the dead and wounded. I heard about Lieutenant Wilfred Funk. He had been shot several times in the back—probably from the tommy gun.

A soldier sharing a foxhole with Jake Tabberaki said that Jake sensed the shooting was friendly fire. He rose to his knees and shouted, "Knock it off!" A bullet immediately smashed through his helmet and into his forehead. I forget the name of the man who told me this, but he was terribly upset. He said that Jake seemed to take forever to die. He would be quiet for several minutes. Then, just when you thought he was gone, a gasp could be heard.

It was late in the day before we realized that we had not found a single dead or wounded enemy soldier. But we were kept on the alert for a couple of days before the truth was acknowledged. The Army Air Corps was right, and the navy had screwed up royally. What happened was this: Army scout aircraft had made repeated low sweeps over Kiska and swore that there were no Japanese left on the island. The navy, positioned offshore, swore with equal vehemence that the enemy could not possibly have slipped by their blockade.

When we landed on the beaches, nobody was recognizable in the fog and mist—hence the so-called friendly fire. But there was plenty of evidence of a hasty Japanese departure—food still on the stoves and a few dogs wandering about. Somehow the enemy, under cover of darkness and fog, had escaped.

While on Kiska, we had every kind of weather except extreme cold—mostly wind-driven rain, and sometimes a williwaw. We lived in tents that often blew down, so Quonset huts were put up. But, we never got to live in them. Our Quonset became the orderly room and mess hall.

My tent had all the oddballs. There was Daniel T. Walsh, bugler; Henry Moscow, editor of our company newspaper, *The Rucksack;* Charlie Graves; and a couple of others whose names I can't remember.

The tents were deployed over a large area and were connected with what was called sound power phones. Just before mess call, Dan would blow a couple of bars of "You Are My Sunshine" on the bugle to get the camp's attention. Then we would do a couple of minutes of in-house comedy—phoney announcements and jokes.

Reginald Pollack and I were the artists for *The Rucksack.* I drew a sketch taking aim at the dehydrated rations we were living on. It was the picture of a can with the label reading "Dehydrated Human (Female) M 1943."

Our diet was lousy. The army probably figured on lots of casualties and was not prepared for so many hungry mouths to feed. Then one day we learned that it was time for the salmon to return. The sight was something to see—salmon, three-feet long, swimming up a stream only inches wide. However, we were not sportsmen. Our fishing technique was quite simple but efficient—throw a concussion grenade (no shrapnel) into one of the shallow ponds, wait for things to settle, then simply pick up the largest stunned fish floating on the surface.

Using a bayonet, we would cut one-inch slices from the center of the salmon and fry them in our mess kits on the tent's stove. Several guys from Company L had an even better idea to catch fish. They would go down to the shore where a small stream flowed into the ocean. At low tide, it flattened out to just a muddy path leading to the water. The powerful urge that influenced the salmon was so strong that they could not wait for the incoming tide; they just laid in the mud and flapped their bodies toward the deeper water of the stream. These Company L sportsmen would wait for a four- or five-pounder, then simply bend down and grab it.

After living a couple of months in this isolated spot, we all became pretty gamey since there were no bathing facilities. Actually, we never noticed the strong aroma because everybody smelled the same. Ted Miller was an inventive sort of wheeler-dealer—the entrepreneur type. He was continually working on various deals, such as lugging in firewood or buckets of coal for a price.

Miller drew up plans for a shower—a Rube Goldberg sort of contraption that involved an elaborate series of buckets and hot water. When it was finished, we all lined up and took makeshift showers. I remember

Dev Jennings emerging so pink and rosy that we didn't recognize him. The upshot of this was that we all came down with bad colds. Maybe it would have been better to remain stinky.

During November, the shrouds we received from the Grave's Registration Department were finally put to good use—for those of us who lived. Thanksgiving was one time when we fussed. We had a table of sorts that Charlie Graves used now and then for his 24-hour bridge games.

For Thanksgiving dinner, we used a clean shroud for a tablecloth, and I lettered individual place cards. The cards were all about three inches long, except for Charlie's. His was longer because, for some reason, I used his full name—Charles Parlin Graves, with a P.F.C. in front of it. The card stood out in the crowd.

Charlie insisted that the navy would be getting the shipment of Thanksgiving turkeys and was going to give the bones to the army. Actually, someone (probably me) started a rumor that we were getting Spam shaped like a turkey. But Charlie was probably closer to the truth. We feasted on canned turkey stew. However, it's amazing what place cards, candles, and table linen can do for class.

CHAPTER 4

Camps Hale and Swift: Prelude to Italy

After the Allied invasion of Sicily on July 9, 1943, the American Fifth and British Eighth Armies battled their way up the bloody boot of Italy. Rome fell eleven months later, but the fighting was far from over. High in the Apennine Mountains, north of Rome, loomed the menacing, heavily fortified Gothic Line. The Allies had made three attempts to break through the German defenses, but all were repulsed.

The 87th Mountain Infantry Regiment returned to Camp Hale in January 1944 and joined the 85th and 86th Mountain Infantry Regiments. Between March 26 and April 15, the ski troops conducted the so-called D-Series of prescribed maneuvers.

The U.S. Army Ground Forces report, *Training for Mountain and Winter Warfare—Study #23*, stated:

> Snow conditions throughout the series were such that two or three feet of snow covered the flat ground at all times. While in the timber, the snow depth was from eight to ten feet. Near the summits of the mountain peaks, drifts forty feet deep were encountered.
>
> The D-Series exercises were completed satisfactorily. The division successfully demonstrated its mastery of tactical and administrative operations under extreme conditions of weather, altitude and terrain.
>
> In addition to its training mission, the ski troops had been directed to test the suitability of their winter and mountain equipment. The results revealed that the division's organization and equipment proved to be so unsatisfactory—and recommended changes so extensive—that the Army Ground Forces suggested that the 10th Light Division be reorganized as a standard division.
>
> Combat reports from Italy indicated that a standard division could be adapted for service in mountainous terrain, while it was still questionable

whether a mountain division could operate efficiently outside of its specialized mission. General George Marshall acknowledged that no firm overseas
requirement had been developed for mountain troops—but he had been
favorably impressed with the potential capabilities of the 10th Light
Division. Marshall directed the Army Ground Forces to make detailed recommendations for the reorganization of the division so that it could more
effectively operate in high altitudes.

Just as the G-3 Section of the Army Ground Forces began its study of proposed changes, the division was transferred, on June 22, to Camp Swift,
Texas. It was scheduled to take part in the September Louisiana maneuvers—and a period of acclimation to a hot climate was deemed necessary.

The ski troops had heard rumors of a possible change to a standard division, and the transfer to Camp Swift seemed to confirm the scuttlebutt.
Their morale began to decline, because they considered themselves a picked
body of men who had been selected for their specialized skills, and they
wanted to fight as a mountain division.

On July 22, the Army Ground Forces submitted its recommendations.
The 10th Light Division would remain a mountain organization. Its strength
was increased by 2,608 officers and enlisted men. The division's deficiency
of firepower was remedied by the activation of a heavy weapons company
for each battalion. Substantial increases were also made in the engineer, signal corps and medical elements. Mule pack transportation was provided for
all combat units of the division—increasing the number of animals to six
thousand.

Incorporating the additional pack animals into the organization—and
familiarizing the troops with their use—was a staggering project. However,
the problem solved itself when the Louisiana maneuvers were canceled due
to the demands of the European Theatre of Operations. This respite gave the
division time to assimilate and train the new men.

On November 6, 1944, the designation of the 10th Light Division was
changed to the 10th Mountain. Later in the month—on Thanksgiving Day—
Major General George P. Hays assumed command of the ski troops.

Sailing orders for the division quickly followed. On December 10, the
86th Regiment embarked aboard the S.S. *Argentina*, and two weeks later
steamed into the harbor at Naples, Italy. The troops were then loaded into
trucks for a short trip to the staging area at Bagnoli. On Christmas Day, the
First Battalion and Headquarters Company motored north to Leghorn.

The following day, the rest of the regiment boarded the Italian freighter
Sestriere and rejoined their fellow ski troopers at Leghorn. The 86th Regiment was then trucked to a staging area near Pisa.

On January 3, 1945, the 85th and 87th Regiments boarded the U.S.S. *West
Point*, arriving at Naples on January 13. Other units of the 10th Mountain
Division sailed aboard the U.S.A.T. *Meigs*, and reached Naples a week later.

CHAPTER 5

The 86th Mountain Infantry Regiment: The Italian Campaign

Located about thirty-five miles north of Florence, the well-entrenched Gothic Line protected Highway 64, the German vital supply route that coiled upward from the Po Valley. The enemy defenses stretched twenty-five miles along the spine of the Apennine Mountains—a series of peaks dominated by the towering and foreboding Mount Belvedere. Situated at a sharp north-south angle to Belvedere was a sheer precipice that would soon etch its name into military history—Riva Ridge.

At the summit of the cliff, four German battalions had an unobstructed view of the valley below, and more than eighty artillery pieces guarded the approaches. In addition, all trails and open areas were heavily mined. The enemy was confident that its mountain fortress was impregnable.

In his self-published booklet FECIT, *edited here with permission, John W. Dewey wrote of his experiences with the 86th Mountain Infantry Regiment.*

In early 1944, I was attached to Company I, 86th Infantry, 10th Mountain Division. We trained in the art of mountain warfare at Camp Hale, Colorado.

During maneuvers, each man carried a rucksack that weighed an average of sixty pounds—consisting of a sleeping bag, shoepac, heavy wool socks, long underwear, a two-man tent, mess kit, one day's K-rations, trench tool, white camouflage suit, and toilet articles—plus skis when not in use.

The weather was severe, with below-zero temperatures at night and blinding blizzards. We froze at night. But, during the day, we sweated from the heat of the hot sun reflecting off the bright white snow.

These maneuvers were the toughest in the army—up one mountain and down another, only to start all over again. We cussed and sweated, not knowing where we were or caring much, either. Mules carried the cookstoves, food, and heavy weapons, but even they gave up at times. The men, however, continued on.

I remember the day when fifteen soldiers and a mule were pulling a machine gun cart up a steep mountain slope through five feet of snow. The mule quit about halfway up, and the men took over, slipping and falling until they reached the summit cold, bruised, and completely exhausted.

There were many nights when the temperature dropped to 35° below zero. On these nights, a soldier did not dare crawl into his sleeping bag. If his body was wet from snow or sweat, he would freeze like an ice cube. On Easter Sunday, we sang "Easter Parade" in a blizzard.

After maneuvers at Camp Hale, orders came through to transfer the 10th Mountain Division to Camp Swift, Texas. This was quite a change from the climate at Colorado—from one extreme to another, typical of army procedure.

The Texas heat got so bad that we worked only at night and rested during the day. For the next couple of months we trained as fast, lightly equipped combat teams. We lived in the field throughout the week but were given weekend passes. Three of us spent one big weekend in Galveston, letting off steam. We did the joints in high style, crashed a beach party, and ended up broke a hundred miles from camp. We spent the next day hitchhiking back to Swift.

More maneuvers followed, but by this time the men had become all too familiar with the broiling sun, burning sand, venomous snakes, and angry scorpions, which could sting like hell and make a man sick to his stomach. Before dressing every morning, we would shake our clothes and turn shoes upside down just to make sure no scorpions were hanging around.

A few times during maneuvers, we camped near a watermelon patch. I imagine there were some farmers who harvested a very poor crop that year.

After our desert exercises had been completed, rumors began to flood the camp. We were going overseas—Burma, the South Pacific, France, and Italy. Each destination was the "official" scuttlebutt. One thing was for sure, though—we were going!

Our convoy sailed from Newport News, Virginia, in December 1944 for Naples, Italy. We were aboard the *Argentina,* a large prewar luxury liner. The men spent most of their time on deck playing cards, writing letters, or just talking. Time passed slowly. Finally, on our sixteenth day at sea, the ship anchored in Naples Harbor. It was night, and all we could see were a few lights sparkling along the shoreline.

Morning dawned bright and clear, giving us a panoramic view of the bay and city. Small boats could soon be seen heading out to our ship.

They were seagoing beggers trying to bum cigarettes and candy from a fresh load of American soldiers.

The *Argentina* docked about noon, and we disembarked. Naples seemed like a teeming mass of noise and confusion, with army vehicles dashing here and there with no apparent destination. The city was filthy. Rubble and squalor were everywhere. The shabbily dressed people were actively going about their daily routine—or stopping to beg from the soldiers.

We were trucked to a camp just outside Naples and billeted in what looked like a college type building. According to local gossip, however, it had been built by Mussolini for the children of the state. The building was an architectural monstrosity. It had been camouflaged and was not damaged by bombing. There were no cots available, so we slept on top of blankets, coats, or anything else we could find to cover the cold, damp floor.

Another soldier and I went to Naples on a pass. It was an eye-opening experience. The city had been ravaged by war, leaving in its wake poverty and starvation. Raggedy young children were running the streets in packs, begging anything they could get from the Americans. Some of the boys were pimping for prostitutes. For a pack of cigarettes, the city was yours.

The houses of prostitution and practically every side street was off limits to our soldiers. Many a drunk GI who lost his way would end up being knifed by a hoodlum, who would take his shoes and clothes and disappear into the darkness.

We took a back-alley "tour" of the real Naples through dark, dimly lighted streets, cobblestone sidewalks, and shabby homes. It began to rain as we hurried to the truck stop to catch our ride back to camp. Places like this make us thankful that we are not fighting on American soil.

A few days later, the Germans were threatening a breakthrough in the mountains above Leghorn. Our regiment was hustled aboard a so-called troop transport, an old steamer that had been confiscated by the U.S. Navy. We were escorted by a couple of potbellied Italian destroyers that looked more like the tugboats flitting about New York Harbor.

We were at sea a day and a night, landed at Leghorn the following morning, and then were taken to a camp several miles north of town. By this time, the German drive had been stopped, but we remained in camp for several days in case we were needed to reinforce our frontline troops.

Off in the distance, we could hear the constant rumble of artillery. It gave us an uneasy feeling. One day, while having our noon meal, there was a nearby explosion. Men dove for cover in every direction. It was "Every man for himself!"

A few minutes later, after things quieted down, we cautiously came out of hiding and checked for damage. It seems that a goat had stepped on a land mine. The owner was crying hysterically over the loss of his precious animal. The relief of tension was electric. We all roared with laughter.

A short time later we received orders to pack up and move out. The regiment went into position northeast of Leghorn—deep in the mountains of the Gothic Line. On our way to the front, the only town I remember passing through was Pisa, with its leaning tower.

My foxhole was an observation post on the point of a pass. It overlooked a valley and the mountains beyond. The valley was a no-man's-land, and the mountains were enemy territory.

Each outpost was occupied, day and night, by two men in four-hour shifts. We watched the Germans, and they watched us. Only patrols were active, probing each other's lines and taking prisoners.

What our patrols feared the most was walking into an ambush. If the men used the same trail more than once, they were sure to meet the Germans lying in wait for them. Usually the men on patrol would be accompanied by a couple of Italian partisans who knew the mountains like the back of their hands.

The first patrol I went out on was surprised by the enemy and had to shoot its way out. We escaped the trap but left one dead soldier and a wounded partisan. We tried to take the wounded man with us, but he refused to hinder our withdrawal.

Newspaper reports constantly referred to Italy as the "quiet front," but every day men were fighting and dying, trying to hold strategic positions until the start of the spring offensive.

The nights were long and very cold. Every sudden sound caused the muscles to tense, and, any moment, we expected to be using our bayonets in hand-to-hand combat. Some men were trigger-happy and shot plenty of holes in the sky before being calmed down.

On the first of February, orders came through to be ready to move out in twenty-four hours. The 86th was being relieved—where it was going, nobody cared. The only thing that mattered was the word "relieved." At dark the next day we boarded trucks and headed south to a rest camp for clean clothes, a much-needed shower, and a chance to receive mail and write letters home.

Mail call had become a welcomed custom in the army. And, when it was over, each soldier went his separate way to read, think, and meditate. Every now and then, the stillness would be broken by the familiar sound of a German 88 or a shout down the line, "I'm a father!"

After a few days of rest and relaxation, we headed back to the front. The trucks drove all day, but the spring thaws had commenced and the trucks soon became bogged down in deep mud. We were forced to abandon the vehicles and continue on foot.

The march was torturous. We trudged all night, mile after mile through tenacious muck, each man carrying a heavy pack.

Many of us were suffering from dysentery and other illnesses. The dysentery caused stomach cramps, nausea, and vomiting. I became very sick and had to drop out of the march. I was picked up by a jeep and taken to regimental headquarters, where I spent the rest of the night.

The 86th Regiment was dug in on a hill opposite the German-held Mount Belvedere. At one time, the partisans had captured this strategic location—but while they were celebrating their victory, the Germans counterattacked and took it back.

American and German patrols were very active, as both sides anticipated the Fifth Army's coming offensive. The weather was cold with rain, sleet, and occasional snow that only added to our misery.

I will never forget the night when eight of us spent the futile hours waiting to ambush an enemy patrol, which two nights earlier had attacked our position and carried off one of our wounded.

I have never been as cold as I was that night, lying flat in the snow, daring not to move or make a sound, my nerves gnawing at my stomach. Even a cough could mean the difference between life and death. Living in no-man's-land is a mixture of fear and maddening revenge. A dead GI, lying nearby, clouds the mind with tears of rage, but a dead German soldier is regarded with contempt.

While on the front line at Mount Belvedere, our squad occupied an abandoned farmhouse. We did not dare venture outside during daylight, as this would draw enemy artillery fire. On one occasion, the building was hit by a shell, but it was a dud and only knocked a few slate shingles off the roof.

We spent the daytime hours sleeping, cleaning rifles, and writing letters home. At night we moved into outpost positions. After about a month, we were pulled off the line and sent to a rear area for showers and clean clothes and to replace any equipment that had been lost or damaged.

Several of us received a one-day pass to Florence, where I sold a carton of cigarettes for fifteen dollars. I bought an Italian billfold, some trinkets, and for my sister a silk scarf.

Florence is a beautiful city, with the ravages of war confined to the outskirts and bridges. We visited the cathedral and saw an American movie in a famous old theater that had been built for operas.

After the show, we had dinner at a restaurant that was operated by the U.S. Army. There was a choice of several dishes, and the meal included a glass of wine. This was luxurious living to men accustomed to C rations and dysentery. Upon returning to camp that night, we were dog-tired and exhausted—but grateful for a day of complete relaxation.

By late February, spring had arrived. The grass was turning green, and flowers were blooming here and there. I began to think of home, but my melancholy mood was soon interrupted. We received orders to be ready to move out in two hours.

On the way to the front, we marched past our troops who had secured the approaches to Mount della Torraccia. The dead and wounded were being carried to the rear. The soldiers, still able to fight, rested in their foxholes—with expressionless eyes staring into empty space. I will never forget the blank, distorted faces of these men—a combination of being scared to hell, tired beyond belief, and shell-shocked.

On the previous day, I watched this battle from a nearby hill and witnessed the murderous effect of German artillery as it cut down men and trees with scythelike efficiency. The enemy had one clear-cut advantage. Whenever they abandoned a position, their artillery kept the location zeroed in.

We went into line on a ridge near the long, flat-topped mountain. Both Mount della Torraccia and Mount Belvedere had to be taken. They were the key approaches to Bologna and northern Italy.

Throughout the night, the Germans—always anticipating an attack—kept taking potshots at us. The sound of erratic gunfire, the sudden scream of a GI shot by a sniper, and the moans of the wounded filled the long, sleepless hours until dawn.

At the first glint of daylight, our artillery opened fire with a thunderous barrage against the enemy. Soldiers who had fallen asleep from nervous exhaustion awoke with a start. For thirty minutes, the big guns pounded the Germans while we moved into position for the attack.

At 0500 hours, the battalion jumped off. Supported by machine guns and mortars, we moved forward up a shallow gully. Enemy artillery answered with devastating accuracy. We took several direct hits. Dead and wounded littered the ground. I stumbled over the body of a German soldier, partly hidden by the tall grass. The sight turned my stomach and made me sick. I raced up the ravine like the devil was after me—half running, half falling—until I reached the top of the gully.

I stopped for a moment to catch my breath and pat a wounded buddy on the back. He had been doing a great job holding down the enemy with a .30-caliber machine gun. Minutes later, he was hit again and killed.

I kept running, following our scouts across the top of the gully and down. We quickly reached a high cliff. It was too steep to climb, so we flanked it to the right. We cautiously worked our way around the bluff until we came to an open area. The terrain sloped up about a hundred yards toward the top of the cliff. Our objective was an enemy machine gun nest operated by two men. The machine gun was holding up our battalion's advance. It had to be knocked out.

Our squad held a conference to decide the best way to attack the German gun. Looking back from this spot, I could see the results of our artillery fire. The bodies of dead and wounded enemy soldiers were lying where they had been shot. Despite their desperate rush to retreat, very few escaped.

Between us and the machine gun was a stone wall two feet high that terraced the hill. From this location, we could watch the German gunners without them seeing us. We figured that a man could crawl within range and fire a rifle grenade. Bob Foster volunteered for the dangerous mission. I covered him with my BAR (Browning automatic rifle). We crept carefully toward the enemy. At about fifty yards from the Germans, Foster fired the grenade. It missed by ten yards. He quickly threw a hand grenade. It landed short, then rolled downhill. Foster hit the dirt as the grenade exploded within a few feet of him.

Gripping his last grenade, Foster sneaked toward the enemy position. When he had safely crawled to within twenty-five feet of the enemy, he pulled the pin and tossed the "bomb." Bull's-eye! Right on target! One German was killed and the other wounded. We immediately secured the position, permitting our flanking units to advance. (For this action, Bob Foster received the Silver Star. John Dewey was awarded the Bronze Star.)

We had safely reached the top of Mount della Torraccia and now found ourselves in the center of a horseshoe-shaped ridge overlooking a valley to the north. We huddled behind the stone wall as protection against enemy small arms fire. Every now and then, one of us would take a quick peek over the wall and shoot at the Germans who were dug in farther down the valley.

One member of our squad was struck by a bullet that tore through his right shoulder blade. We treated the gaping wound with sulfa powder, covered him with a blanket, and shouted for a medic. Because of the large number of wounded, however, it was more than an hour before a medic was able to get to us.

When another man poked his head over the wall to take a shot at the Germans, an enemy bullet smashed through his helmet. It grazed his forehead, making him temporarily raving mad. We had to hold the soldier down to stop him from climbing over the wall to get at the Germans.

Throughout the morning, we defended our position against murderous enemy fire. Six of us held three hundred yards of the ridge, but our right flank was exposed. The minutes passed lonely and desperately. It was about noon before Mount della Torraccia was secured and reserve units were brought up. It was a great feeling of relief to have a solid line of our troops digging in on the reverse side of the horseshoe. As the new men moved into position, they asked about their friends. Some had been wounded and others killed.

The medics were busy long after the fighting had stopped, taking care of the severely wounded first, then coming back to the less seriously injured. It is dangerous work being an infantryman. But the medic—unarmed and exposed to enemy fire—has the toughest job of all.

One of my close friends had been struck in the head by shrapnel. He lay on the ground all day—semiconscious—with part of his brain bulging out from his skull. While waiting for litter bearers, he was exposed to enemy fire and continually showered with dirt from nearby shell bursts. It was a frustrating and sickening sight. Even after a shot of morphine, he would moan and roll about in terrible agony. It took a long time for him to die.

Amid all this horror and death, I stumbled over the body of a little girl who had been killed during the morning exchange of artillery fire. She was lying near a hedgerow where she had fallen in a desperate flight to escape exploding shells. At the sight of her broken, lifeless figure, I was reminded of my seven-year-old sister. I cried until tears would not come anymore. I carefully picked the child up in my arms and carried her to the rear, where Graves Registration could locate her family and she could be given a decent burial.

Early that night, the Germans launched a series of counterattacks, one wave after another. We hunkered down in foxholes as enemy artillery pounded our positions. The shelling was followed by a short period of ominous silence. Then, suddenly, our fieldpieces opened fire with a thunderous barrage of timed shells that exploded just above ground. Hot shrapnel mowed down the advancing enemy. The Germans who did manage to reach our lines surrendered.

The following day was comparatively quiet with only an occasional exchange of artillery and mortar fire. We spent most of the time digging deeper foxholes. A dugout, about five feet deep, seemed safe enough during the day. But at night, living under the menace of German artillery, we felt like we were five feet above ground.

In the afternoon, we were told to be ready to go out on a night patrol. The mission would be to establish contact with Brazilian troops on our right flank.

Those of us assigned to this patrol were eagerly looking forward to getting away from the enemy attacks. But, upon reporting to battalion headquarters, we learned that the orders had been changed. There was a shortage of litter bearers, and we were told to take some litters and help collect the dead. I was shocked by the order. Asking a man to fight is one thing, but asking him to pick up the bloodied bodies of his friends is another.

We were handed a rope, and I quickly learned why. The first body I placed on a litter had been a member of my platoon. He lay where he had fallen—cold, stiff, and bent over clutching his stomach. Trying to carry a body in this rigid position was impossible. Unless it was tied down, it would roll off the litter.

It was no sooner dark than German artillery opened fire again. As I hurried to take cover, I passed a buddy in a forward foxhole. He had been shaken up by an exploding shell and was afraid that the next one might get him. He asked me if I wanted to trade jobs. Anything to get off the morgue detail, I decided, and agreed to the switch.

I soon discovered, however, that this foxhole was on the front slope of the horseshoe and faced the enemy lines. The night was quiet for a few minutes, then all hell broke loose. German artillery had zeroed in on the slope. No wonder my "friend" had been so eager to trade.

Moments later, a shell crashed into the embankment in front of me and exploded. I was slammed to the ground and covered with dirt. With my ears still ringing from the blast, I took off running for the reverse slope of the horseshoe. I never ran so fast in my life. It was the superhuman speed of a man crazed with fear. I tumbled across the slope and into my old foxhole. It was already occupied by two men. I scrambled out and kept running. By this time I was frantic, but I finally found a dugout with only one occupant—our first lieutenant. I did not ask permission—I just jumped in.

The artillery duel continued for five hours, both sides firing without letup. The noise was deafening—almost maddening. Somewhere below us, we could hear the screams of a shell-shocked soldier and the cries of the wounded.

The morning dawned clear and warm. The artillery battle had ceased, and an uneasy quiet pervaded the battleground. Luckily, not a man in my platoon had been killed, despite the accuracy of enemy fire. After being kept awake all night, we dozed off most of the day from sheer exhaustion, but we were too edgy and nervous to sleep very long.

My foxhole was near the machine gun nest we had knocked out earlier. The dead German had not yet been buried and was starting to smell. The nauseating odor of decaying flesh cannot be described. A few of us pushed the body into a hastily dug hole and covered it with dirt. We marked the spot with the dead soldier's helmet. The Graves Registration men would later dig up the body and take it to a military cemetery.

Several days later, we were told to be ready to move out early the next morning. Once again, the fear of actual combat numbed the senses. You never get used to it. The nerve-racking thought that some of us might not live through the next attack was ever present. A number of men had premonitions that they would not survive the action. More often than not, they were right.

I awoke an hour before jump-off time. The mountains were shrouded in thick fog. I wondered how men could fight under these conditions, but the mist soon cleared and once more we were on the move. P-47 Thunderbolts supported our attack, softening up the enemy positions with bombs, rockets, and machine gun fire.

We were only able to advance a few hundred yards at a time before being stopped by strong German defenses. As darkness settled, we dug in to the newly won positions. By now, however, our casualties were creating many empty spaces in the ranks. Eight-man squads had been reduced to four or five. Replacements were supposedly on the way, but when they would arrive was anybody's guess.

The following day, Company I was in reserve, and it was our job to send captured enemy soldiers to the rear and immobilize any of their equipment not already destroyed. We passed our regimental commander, who had been shot in the arm by a sniper. When asked how he was feeling, the colonel replied, "Fine—that Kraut was a damn poor shot!"

The regiment gained five miles, and at dusk Company I relieved the troops who had been fighting all day. We occupied the newly won positions and prepared to lead the next morning's attack.

During the evening, the artillery moved up to give us close support. But the Germans had the position perfectly zeroed in, and after an aid station and one gun battery took direct hits, our artillery was moved back behind a ridge.

We had just dug in and were eating our C rations when orders were issued to prepare to pack up. As soon as it became dark, we were to proceed to a new forward area. Later that night, the enemy—not knowing we had relocated the line—continued to shell our old position.

The next day, our attack was again bitterly contested. But, despite stubborn resistance, we pushed ahead two miles and captured a strategic ridge overlooking a large L-shaped valley. A main German supply route cut through the valley, and our command of the heights restricted their troop and supply movements. The enemy, however, was able to observe us from two sides, and this made it almost impossible to move about in the daylight without drawing artillery fire.

I dug my foxhole into the side of the hill and encircled it with a stone wall about two feet high. This afforded protection against shrapnel and permitted me to observe enemy movements through peepholes in the wall.

Our company had reached the ridge early in the afternoon, giving us plenty of time before dark to secure our positions. One GI noticed a pair of boots on top of the ridge. He carefully crept up and tried to grab them, but they would not budge. The Germans had hurriedly buried one of their dead, leaving only his feet sticking out from the shallow grave.

An enemy sniper was hiding somewhere below the ridge, taking pot-shots at any man who showed himself. Then, during the night, several Germans climbed the steep cliffs and began shooting at anything that moved. We managed to drive them off with grenades and mortar fire.

The next day, another soldier and I were using field glasses to search for enemy positions. But, inadvertently, I moved my binoculars too fast, and sunlight reflected off the lens that—acting like a mirror—exposed our location. We quickly realized what had happened and knew all hell would be breaking loose any minute. We huddled down in our foxhole to sweat out the imminent artillery barrage. The first enemy shell exploded on our left, the second to the right. The Germans were bracketing our location. The next shell exploded so close that we were covered with rocks and dirt. Then came a short pause followed by the sound of a distant gun being fired. We braced ourselves for the blast but only heard a dull thud in front of the foxhole. An eternity seemed to pass, but there was no explosion. We got the hell out and ran for the safety of a bluff. Evidently the Germans figured they had made a direct hit, as the firing ceased.

At twilight, we returned to our foxhole to check where the last shell had landed. I found it buried in the ground, not five feet from my observation post and directly in line with the very peephole I had been using. It was as though God had interceded, and a silent prayer of thanks acknowledged my appreciation. A few days later, our regiment was relieved and we were sent back to a temporary camp well behind the lines.

For the troops on the front line, life is grim, dirty, and dangerous. They are seldom, if ever, familiar with the grand strategy of the division commander, nor do they know how the units on each flank are progressing. Every soldier knows his company's objective, but the soldier himself is only concerned with the man to his immediate left and right—and so on down the line.

With each dash toward the enemy, the soldier prays for his life, hoping he will reach cover before he is killed or wounded. An infantryman lives from second to second running, crouching, and falling while still hoping to get a shot off at the enemy.

Each GI keeps in contact with a buddy, letting nothing short of death come between them. Through dust, smoke, and thundering artillery, the soldier must push forward.

Men do strange things in war, living more like animals than human beings. All the teachings of modern civilization are abandoned to the barbaric ways of self-preservation. We hated it. The enemy hated it. But we were at war with each other. In peacetime, you get the electric chair for killing. In wartime, you get a medal.

On July 10, 1943, Lloyd Fitch landed on the beaches of Sicily as a member of the U.S. 45th Division. He was later assigned to the 86th Mountain Infantry Regiment of the 10th Mountain Division as an infantry replacement. Lloyd Fitch's memoirs give a vivid account of life and death on the front lines.

I joined the army in December 1942 and received my basic training in Mississippi. In June 1943, my outfit left New York with a convoy bound for Africa. The ship was small—almost as tall as it was long—and top-heavy.

We were on the ocean about a week when we ran into rough water. Practically everyone was seasick. My buddy, H. A. Newton, and I were eating breakfast one morning while high waves were bouncing the ship. We had to hold our food trays or they would slide off the table. Soldiers were vomiting all over the tables and deck. Newton was about to swallow a hunk of bacon when the fellow sitting next to him threw up all over Newt's mess tray. I thought my buddy was about to lose his breakfast also, but he managed to keep it down.

By this time, we had enough of cruise-ship grub and decided to get some fresh air. But walking on a slippery deck was difficult. The ship would sway one way, then the other. The guys who didn't keep their balance would fall backwards into the slop.

In order to pass the time on this boring voyage and bring a little excitement into our lives, Newt and I would climb up to the third deck, lean over the rail, make loud vomiting sounds, and pour a little canteen water onto the lower decks. The men below us would stumble over each other trying to escape the spray. We had a lot of laughs over this.

I remember one evening, about sunset, when a German submarine was sighted. Escorting destroyers dropped several depth charges, and we changed course a couple of times. A pessimistic fellow in our group said, "I'll never come back alive anyway!" and tossed all his money overboard.

After about two weeks at sea, we docked at Oran, Algeria. I was surprised to see the harbor swarming with American troops and vehicles. My introduction to African culture occurred when an Arab squatted on the dock, relieved himself, then wiped his bottom with his long shirt. Back home you would get arrested for this.

We soon steamed to a beach for maneuvers and training. We had to run an obstacle course, and I was determined to be the first man in my company to complete it. The course was difficult and dangerous. I had to jump up, grab the side of a wall, climb over the top, grasp a rope, then swing across a ditch filled with barbed wire. I landed safely. But one soldier didn't quite make it and swung backwards into the sharp metal barbs.

Sicily was the next stop on our "Mediterranean tour." Once again, the sea was rough and nearly everybody was sick. We arrived off the Sicilian coast on the early morning of July 10. The waves were high, and the navy coxswains had trouble maneuvering their boats. The landing craft bounced like corks, banging hard against the side of our ship. Rope nets were lowered, and the first sergeant and I climbed down to one of the craft, then held the nets for other men to keep them from being crushed as the small boats slammed repeatedly against the steel bulkheads of the transport.

When my unit landed, we were immediately put to work loading trucks with ammunition already stacked along the shore. At one point on the beach, we discovered a number of full wine casks. They were large barrels and probably held at least two hundred gallons of wine each. Some of the boys shot holes in the casks, and anyone who had a thirst for vino filled their canteen or cup before moving on. It wasn't a strong wine, but any soldier drinking a liter or so would feel the effects.

A few nights later, I witnessed one of the tragedies of the war. A number of C-47s, towing gliders loaded with members of the 82nd Airborne Division, took off from Africa and headed for Sicily to support our ground troops.

Earlier that day, German bombers attacked our beachhead and sank a British hospital ship and an American ammunition vessel. More air raids were anticipated, and all gunners were put on high alert. About midnight—just before the airborne troops arrived—enemy planes launched another attack on our invasion fleet but were driven off.

We were still firing rounds into the sky when the slow-flying C-47s were spotted coming in at seven hundred feet. They were immediately taken for German aircraft and were met with a barrage of gunfire. It was a slaughter. More than three hundred of our paratroopers were killed, and their bodies kept floating to shore for days.

Another time, while we were unloading ammunition, a plane flew over a hill and raced down the beach. Our antiaircraft crews reacted with split second precision, swinging their guns around and firing at point-blank range. The plane seemed to halt in midair from the impact of striking a wall of shells. It dropped like a rock, slammed into the ground about fifty yards from me, and burst into flames. The scorching blaze set off the aircraft's ammunition. Bullets flew in all directions. We had to wait until the fires died out before it was safe to approach the smouldering wreck.

A few of us carefully crept up on the plane and discovered it was one of ours. The American pilot's body had been burnt to a crisp. If you poked a finger into his arm, it would probably go clear to the bone. The sudden realization that we had shot down one of our own aircraft was unnerving, I have never forgotten the incident.

The Italian soldiers soon began surrendering in droves. They weren't too anxious about fighting this war anyway. I remember the pitch-black night when I was one of several guards escorting a large group of prisoners along the beach. Suddenly a group of enemy planes raced in over the hills. The Italians dropped flat on the ground. In order to move from one side of the column to the other, I had to walk across a carpet of human bodies. As we headed up the shore toward Scoglitti, I began to wonder where the guards ahead of and behind me were located. I slowed down for five minutes but never did find another guard covering the rear. This was unusual, so I figured that I had better hurry and catch up with the guy in front. I walked as fast as I could for about ten minutes but didn't see him. I later learned that only eighteen of us were escorting thirteen hundred Italian and six German prisoners. It was like leading a herd of cows up the road. A couple of the Germans escaped in the dark.

When we reached Palermo, I became ill with malaria and was transferred to a British hospital ship for evacuation to Bizerte, Tunisia. The vessel was painted white and, with all its lights on, made a tempting target for enemy aircraft and submarines. But we arrived safely, and as the hospital ship steamed into the harbor, the masts of more than a dozen sunken vessels—both Allied and German—could be seen.

I was sent to a military hospital a few miles inland. Practically every night, enemy aircraft would race in and bomb the stuffings out of the harbor. When searchlights probing the night sky locked on a German plane, it would immediately be caught in the glare of light from our ship and riddled with antiaircraft fire. I remember one plane that was trapped in the lights. It suddenly disappeared from view, but seconds later it crashed into a distant cliff and burst into flames.

Some of the German planes would dive-bomb the ships. About every fifth antiaircraft shell was a tracer, and you could see them come up and meet the enemy head-on. The planes that survived our bullets and shrapnel would drop a bomb or two and then escape. Others would go into a dive and never come out of it. The earth trembled from the impact of an aircraft crashing with a full bomb load. The action was really something to see. It was like watching a movie.

Speaking of movies, I remember the night when several hundred of us were relaxing on the side of a hill watching a John Wayne film. I had managed to get ahold of a bottle of wine and shared it with another soldier who had been shell-shocked. In the middle of the show, one of our planes flew over without identifying itself. Searchlight beams quickly picked it up. That's all my shell-shocked friend needed to see. He began screaming, "Air raid! Air raid! Air raid!" The movie stopped. Men stampeded in all directions. I tried to shut the guy up, but he just kept hollering and creating more panic.

Upon my release from the hospital, I rejoined my company at Palermo, Sicily. Newt caught me up on all the news. He told me about the air raids that he had been through while I was gone. One night, while Newt was with a work party unloading a ship in the harbor, enemy planes raced in and bombed a nearby transport. The ship immediately took on a sharp list and looked like it would capsize. One of the sailors jumped over the side. He dropped down between the transport and the ship next to it. But the bombed vessel did not turn all the way over. It quickly righted itself and must have mashed the fellow, because Newt said he never saw the sailor again.

Newt also remarked that the air attack did not bother him as much as one soldier who gripped his shoulder and, shaking like a leaf, kept repeating, "We're going to be all right, aren't we, Newt? We're not going to be bombed, are we? We'll be all right, won't we?" Newt told me that he could stand the air raid, but this guy almost drove him up a wall.

We had captured several enemy vehicles, and were now able to ride for a change. I was sitting on the front seat of one of the trucks when several American planes flew over us. Evidently, they assumed we were Germans. The first aircraft zoomed across our convoy with all guns firing. By the time the second plane attacked, I had jumped off the truck and dived into a ditch alongside the road. Luckily, it wasn't mined. The pilot in the next plane recognized us as Americans. He wigwagged his wings and flew away. A few of my friends were wounded by machine gun bullets.

Newt and I had another close call one night outside Palermo. We were with several trucks near an ammunition dump when German aircraft appeared and dropped flares and bombs. They apparently knew where the dump was located and hit it right on the bull's-eye. What a sight! Shells exploded everywhere, and there were no foxholes around. We dashed for cover behind the wheels of a truck. Shrapnel and bullets zipped on all sides of us. We lived through the fireworks, but there were some hair-raising moments.

We had been in Sicily for about a year when our quartermaster battalion moved across the Messina Strait to Italy. Our outfit was then broken up and sent to different units for infantry training.

One day during training, Newt and I sneaked over to a Scots encampment. We visited with the troops and drank some of their native beer. It must have been stronger than our American brew, because we got pretty tanked up.

It was late at night by the time we returned to our area. Both of us were hungry and decided to sneak into the darkened mess hall and get something to eat. We grabbed some eggs and bread, but as we slipped out of the kitchen we were spotted by a guard and ordered to halt. Newt ran and got away, but I stopped. I wasn't too keen about getting a bullet in the back.

I was marched to my company headquarters for punishment. I explained to the duty officer that I was just hungry and looking for something to eat. I was ordered to report to the first sergeant every fifteen minutes, from 6 to 10 P.M., for a week.

Newt managed to reach our barracks without being caught. He jumped into bed—clothes and all—and dropped flat on his stomach. But he had forgotten about the eggs in his pockets. The next morning when he awoke, he automatically reached for his cigarettes and lighter. All he pulled out, however, was a mess of crushed, stringy eggs. We both learned the hard way that crime doesn't pay—even in the army.

Upon finishing infantry training, we were transferred to the 86th Mountain Infanty Regiment, 10th Mountain Division, as replacements for the dead and wounded. For some reason, I was assigned to be first scout rifleman, which meant that I would be the regiment's first soldier to enter a town—not the safest job in a war.

When we arrived at the front, the American line was north of Florence, not too many miles from the Po Valley. It was late at night when we reached our sector. Ammunition and grenades were issued to us, and we occupied previously dug bunkers.

At daylight, I noticed that we were positioned near the top of a high ridge with the Germans below us. While we were busy familiarizing ourselves with our new surroundings, several British soldiers came up to us and said they were going to set fire to a few buildings and haystacks down in the valley. We were also warned that German artillery would reply to the bombardment so we had better keep low.

The Brits launched a number of mortar shells, burning the haystacks. The enemy quickly returned fire, and it was accurate. One shell exploded near my dugout, filling it with clouds of sand and dirt. The dust was so thick that I could hardly breathe. Unfortunately, I had placed my field pack and boots outside on the ground. They were riddled with shrapnel.

From this location, we took our lives in our hands to get any food and water. We had to run up the slope and then down the back side of the hill. Any slowpokes came under enemy fire. Some soldiers refused to leave their dugout during daylight hours.

After a few days, I was moved to a new dugout, which I shared with another soldier. This guy kept losing his false teeth, hoping he would be taken off the front line. There was one night when we both were overly tired. We took turns being on watch and relieved each other quite frequently. On one occasion, when it was his turn to take over the watch, I remarked that the trees to our front seemed to be moving—but I was so sleepy, I couldn't be absolutely sure. Well, that was all this fellow had to hear. I was just about to doze off when he suddenly kicked me awake and began shouting, "They're coming! They're coming! The Germans are right out there! Can you see them?! Can you see them?!" I jumped up from a half-sleep and hollered to our sergeant about two dugouts away, "We got some Germans down here! What do you want us to do?" After a few choice remarks about being awakened, he yelled, "Kill them!" So, obeying orders, we opened fire.

At daylight, we saw that there were no enemy soldiers dead on the ground—only a bunch of trees shot full of holes. The sergeant decided that we were the two most incompetent soldiers in the U.S. Army to be sharing a dugout.

My new dugout mate was Hernandez. He was a Mexican fellow from Colorado and one of the bravest men I have ever known. After a few days of nightmarish living under a steady stream of artillery fire—both ours and theirs—we never knew what was going to happen next.

One artillery spotter radioed his battery whenever enemy shells were coming over, and the gun crews would run for cover. But, you're never actually safe out here. There was one gunner who phoned the spotter that a German shell had plowed into the ground in front of his bunker but did not explode. He barely got the words out of his mouth when the shell went off, killing him and another soldier.

Just before the Po Valley push, a group of us were driven to a rest camp about five miles behind the lines. When I returned to my company after a couple of days, I managed to get a twelve-hour pass. But, it had been a long time since I was given a pass of any kind, so I decided to extend my freedom for thirty-six hours. The first sergeant was mad as hell when I came back. He shoved a shovel into my hands and shouted that I would be digging straddle trenches until the end of the war. Fortunately for me, the Po Valley campaign was about to begin, and I was ordered back to the front lines.

This sergeant and a lieutenant did not appreciate replacement soldiers like myself. I had heard them remark, "Fitch will last about three minutes on the Po Valley push." It hurt my feelings to hear them to talk about me that way. But within two days after the attack began, both of them had been wounded, and I was still alive and well.

Crossing the Po Valley, we walked, ran, and crawled fifty-five miles in two days. Whenever we came to farmhouse, the call would be "Scouts out!" That was me. I would make a dash to the building, check for Germans, then run back to my column.

A number of tanks supported our advance. One soldier was walking too near the gun barrel of a tank when it fired a shell. The concussion blew out his eardrums. He was shell-shocked and ended up in a psychiatric hospital in the States.

One time, as we approached a hill, a German tank was observed positioned in what was left of a house. Two walls were standing. Our squad leader, Sergeant Sullivan shouted, "Down! Everybody down!" Just as we hit the dirt, the Germans opened fire. Sullivan was shot. Our lieutenant ordered one of the new replacements to go out and check on the sergeant. The young kid was scared to death and kept repeating, "I don't know! I don't know! I don't want to see!" The lieutenant demanded that he had better go and find out. So, the kid crawled over to Sullivan. He reported back that the sergeant had been hit in the abdomen, and the bullet had come out his tailbone. The soldier also said that he stayed with Sullivan for about fifteen minutes, listening to his moaning and groaning until it finally stopped.

Meanwhile, we were still pinned down by the tank. The lieutenant told us that he would go back to company headquarters and get some mortar fire directed at the German. However, he only went about five hundred yards to the rear and just stayed there, leaving us with the tank looking down our throats.

One of our platoon sergeants told me to sneak around the other side of the hill and deliver a message to a platoon waiting there. I crawled and ran until I reached the troops. I explained our situation to them and that they were to attack the enemy from their side of the hill while we hit the Germans from our location.

I made it safely back to my outfit only to learn that we were not going to take the hill right then. I was mad as hell. I could have been killed. I told the sergeant—in no uncertain terms—that somebody had better tell the boys on the other side of the hill, because they were ready to go.

We hunted for our lieutenant and found him about a hundred yards to the rear—not doing anything or helping us out in any way. The sergeant was boiling mad and shouted at the officer, "Don't you ever leave me in a spot like this again!"

Sarge must have really frightened the lieutenant. He was scared to death and promised never to leave us in the lurch again. He didn't have to. He was shot in the next action.

Another time, while advancing under heavy enemy artillery fire, we stumbled upon a small spring. A pipe was leading from the water to a drinking trough for animals. German shelling was so accurate that the ground was shaking, and water flowed from the pipe in spurts instead of a continuous stream. I stopped to fill my canteen, then hurried to catch up with my squad.

We soon entered a level area between two ridges. Enemy artillery had the high ground and opened fire on us. We scattered and hit the dirt. Each shell that exploded near me felt like it was ripping the skin off my back. There were no foxholes to jump into, and no time to dig one. All we could do was just hug Mother Earth and pray.

I noticed that our sergeant was busy taking care of a wounded friend. It must have been about fifteen minutes before he ordered us to escape over to the reverse slope of a hill, where we would be hidden from view of the Germans. Later, when an officer asked the sergeant why he had kept us under fire so long, the sergeant said that he was helping a buddy who had been shot. The officer really chewed him out for risking all our lives for one man.

Since I was a replacement—and also first scout—it seemed that I was always called upon to take the greatest risks. There was a well near the top of this one hill, and the sergeant told Richard Stanyck and me to get water. We loaded up all the empty canteens we could carry and headed up the slope.

There were already eight soldiers from a tank company in line as the bucket was dropped down the well and hauled up. As we were filling our canteens, one of the tank men was evidently in a hurry. He angrily remarked, "I'm moving closer!" and pushed the man in front of him away from the well. A moment later, a German shell hit. The force of the explosion knocked everyone to the ground, killing the man who had been pushed.

I shouted to Stanyck, "Are you OK?" He answered, "Yes!" I said, "Let's get the hell out of here!" We grabbed the canteens and ran down the hill like the devil was after us. When we reached our platoon, I threw the canteens—some empty, some full—to the men. I tossed one canteen to the sergeant and hollered, "You're thirstier than I am. The next time you want water, go get it yourself!" He never made any more demands on me after that.

One afternoon, while dug in on the top of a hill, we set up a machine gun nest and flares with a trip-wire about a hundred yards down the slope. Since it was still daylight, some of the boys were permitted to go around to nearby farmhouses to try to scrounge up some food and wine. However, they were cautioned not to go very far and to be back before dark.

Meanwhile, we were all keyed up, expecting a German counterattack from the north. Shortly after dark, the wire was tripped. A flare shot off, and the machine gun cut loose. Suddenly there was a cry, "Don't shoot! Don't shoot! Please don't shoot!"

Our squad leader called out in German for the stranger to come forward. As the man approached our lines everyone was on the alert, expecting an English-speaking German leading a group of enemy troops. We were stunned when the guy turned out to be one of our own men. He had been out searching for food and became lost. The kid was shaking so much that he could hardly talk. A nearby officer grabbed the soldier, shook him, and told him to get back to his company and not to leave it until the war was over. The fellow was so frightened that I bet he obeyed that order to the letter.

From then on, it was frontline duty until the end of the war. In fact, as first scout, I was the first American to enter most of the towns. However, being first scout was more like being "first target."

I remember the time when the battalion's first scout and I were checking some enemy bunkers. We found one with a few Germans still inside. We told them to come out, or we would have to fire into the dugout. Just as they were about to exit, I heard a voice behind me announce in broken English, "I surrender!"

I almost jumped out of my skin and never turned around so fast in my life. There stood a German soldier with his arms raised. Fortunately, he was surrendering. I could have been shot in the back.

As we pushed deeper into the Po Valley, the enemy began giving up in large numbers. Most of the time we could not afford to send them to the rear under guard, which would cut down on the amount of troops needed on the front line. So we would round up the prisoners, take their weapons and ammunition away, and send them to the rear unescorted. At times we would fire a couple of rounds over their heads to hurry them up. Some of our soldiers would take watches, rings, and other valuables off the prisoners as war souvenirs.

One day, while on the attack, we stopped in a grove of trees and dug foxholes. They were not very deep, since we figured that orders to move out could come at any time. It turned out to be a very dangerous spot. The Germans had zeroed in on us and began firing mortar shells into the trees. Hot shrapnel was flying in all directions. It's times like this when you wish there was a roof over your foxhole—or else that you had dug it deeper. We lucked out, however; nobody in our squad was hit.

I had another hair-raising experience during the Po Valley campaign. As our advance continued, we came upon a farmhouse with bars on the windows. I, being first scout, went to check it out. I carefully approached the building and called out a few words I knew in Italian. There was no answer. I hurried back to my squad and told the sergeant that I was going to throw a hand grenade through one of the windows.

I don't know why I volunteered. I was deathly afraid of grenades, and had twisted the cotter pins around so they wouldn't come loose in the grenade bag.

I returned to the farmhouse, quickly pulled the key on a grenade, and tossed it at a window. It hit one of the bars, bounced back, and landed at my feet. My reaction was automatic. I can't recall ever moving so fast. I grabbed the grenade, shoved it through the window, and hit the dirt just as it exploded.

I didn't realize it at first, but a few members of my squad were standing near me and could have been killed or wounded. To this day, I believe that the good Lord added a couple of seconds to the timer on that grenade.

As we pushed on toward Verona, a number of tanks joined us. I rode on the first tank that entered the city. Most of the Germans had already left, but a few rear guard units remained and had to be cleaned out.

We chased the enemy to a large lake, Lake Garda, and now had reached the foothills of the Alps. Our progress was slowed, however, by a series of blocked tunnels along the shore of the lake. We had to crawl over bodies, vehicles, and debris to make our way through the clogged passages.

Whenever we exited a tunnel and were out in the open, the Germans would spray us with mortar and machine gun fire from the opposite shore. Their guns also pounded the high cliffs above our heads, causing an avalanche of rocks to cascade down on us. We didn't waste any time running between tunnels.

German artillery had blasted a hole in the side of one tunnel, and we were like clay pigeons to enemy gunners as we dashed across the rubble-filled opening.

At dusk, we climbed aboard amphibious "ducks" and were landed up the coast at Torbole. At one point, while fighting our way into town, we crept alongside a four-foot-high cement wall. We were under heavy enemy fire and jumped over the wall to escape the bullets.

The sergeant and I were lying flat on the ground about ten feet from a large tree. Suddenly a German shell struck the base of the tree and exploded. The force of the blast lifted me up off my right elbow and slammed me back to the ground. I wasn't injured, but the sergeant was blinded. He jumped up and began staggering around. Martinez grabbed him and pulled him out of the line of fire.

Martinez was one of the bravest men I have ever known. He had a kid brother who had been killed fighting the Germans and was determined to avenge his death. I remember the day he escorted three enemy soldiers to the rear echelon command post. They never arrived. But when Martinez returned, he had a satisfied look on his face. I never questioned him about it.

We continued cleaning out pockets of enemy resistance. We entered Riva without opposition and were greeted with cheers and shouts from the crowds lining both sides of the street.

When the war in Europe ended, we were sent into the Alps to prevent any enemy troops from escaping to Austria. As we headed toward the mountains, surrendered German soldiers lined both sides of the road. They still carried their weapons, and it was sort of unnerving to pass by hundreds of armed enemy troops moving to the rear.

I was awarded four battle stars for my service in Africa and Italy. As for wounds, I didn't receive any Purple Hearts, but I was wounded while on the front lines. I cut my right forefinger opening a cheese K ration. And, while in Sicily, I was sharpening a stick with a captured Italian bayonet when it slipped and jabbed me in the leg.

The course of any war runs a whirlpool gauntlet of human experience from horror to humor. Tony Hyde's recollections are no exception.

I had been a second lieutenant for about six months when I arrived at Camp Hale in the summer of 1943. Officers were in short supply, and I was placed in command of Company D, 86th Mountain Infantry Regiment. In preparation for the coming winter, we were issued ski boots and ski poles. Much to my surprise, the skis and bindings were separate. It was assumed that we would attach the bindings ourselves. But, although most of us had skied before, it was on store-bought skis. The problem was quickly solved however, and the skis were ready in a few days.

Our ski boots—at least the army's conception of ski boots—were leather and consisted of two types. One style was snug-fitting and made a pretty good boot. The other was bulky and cumbersome but permitted extra pairs of socks, and supposedly warmer feet. Needless to say, the experienced skiers selected the tighter boot, while those who didn't know any better chose the fatter model.

All went well until overnight training exercises began and we started camping out. As campers have done ever since some caveman discovered fire, the men gathered around the evening fire and warmed their feet. The following day, the soldier's feet would again become cold and wet. But at night—in front of the hot flames—they would soon be warm and dry.

A boot left out in the weather at night would freeze as hard as a block of wood. Putting it on the next morning was very painful, if not impossible. One solution was to take the boots into the sleeping bag with you and try to sleep with them held tightly against your chest.

After about a month of daily soaking and nightly toasting, the soles of the boots began to develop cracks. No problem—just take them to the supply room, show the obviously "defective" boots to the sergeant, and get issued a new pair. By the time spring rolled around, the pile of boots in a corner of the supply room had reached chest height.

It wasn't long before someone at army headquarters discovered that our battalion had been issued more ski boots than we had men. This "scandal" resulted in a new directive that anyone found with cracked boots would have to pay for new ones.

At this same time, I was selected to go to Company Commanders school at Fort Benning, Georgia. As I was getting organized to leave, I was approached by the supply sergeant. He showed me the pile of boots and asked me if I had any ideas on what to do with them. He said that there was really no record of them, but if someone from army headquarters showed up and saw the boots, there would be an investigation. And, since I was driving to Georgia in my old beat-up Plymouth, he suggested I take them with me. Instant solution. Boots? What boots?

The sergeant and I stuffed the damaged boots in mattress covers, packed them into the back seat of the Plymouth, and I headed for Georgia. Driving south from Camp Hale, I planned to visit New Orleans since I had never been to the city. My route took me through New Mexico and Texas. I saw plenty of rugged country but no convenient gully or canyon that could swallow up a couple hundred pairs of ski boots.

When I reached the Mississippi delta country, however, there were plenty of streams, rivers, and bayous—each crossed by a bridge. My problem was solved. Upon reaching the middle of each bridge, I tossed out a boot or two. But then it dawned on me that if I threw out a pair of the same size, someone might find the boots and wear them. This could result in embarrassing questions. To prevent this possibility, I would get rid of a few right boots and then a like number of lefts. By the time I reached Alabama, the only thing I had in my back seat were empty mattress covers. There was no sign of a ski boot anywhere. Company D was in the clear.

I was the commanding officer of Company M when our regiment arrived at Pisa, Italy, in January 1945. After a couple of weeks of unpacking, cleaning weapons, taking a few hikes on local roads, and a bit of training, we received orders to relieve some Allied units at the front. At a company commander's meeting, I learned that we were to take over from a British outfit near Bagni de Lucca.

The left flank of our position was located in a small village just north of Bagni de Lucca. There was no road to the village, only a graded path paved with flat stones and steps at the steeper sections.

The next day, my messenger and I hiked up the path to speak with the British. We needed to know the location of their artillery so that when we relieved them the following night, we would know where to place our guns.

The village—all eight houses—appeared to be deserted. But we soon found a British soldier and asked him where their headquarters was located. He pointed to a white house across the street and said that the officers were probably inside having lunch.

Upon entering the building, I heard voices emanating from the second floor. We carefully climbed the stairs. I knocked on a door and was asked to come in. To our astonishment, we saw several British officers seated around a table covered with a white cloth and upon which were glassware and utensils. Having just come from living in a tent and eating out of a mess kit, I was completely surprised at this sight.

I introduced myself, was greeted warmly, and immediately offered a drink. When I asked what a "drink" might be, the answer was gin and tonic—no ice. This kind of drink was new to us, but I learned early in life never to look a gift horse in the mouth. We said that gin and tonic would be just fine.

About an hour later, I mentioned to our hosts that it might be a good idea if we could have a look at their positions before it became too dark. The captain of the British detachment assured me that there was plenty of time but agreed to my wishes. He appointed an officer to be our guide.

We followed our escort past a couple of houses, across a small meadow, and up a knoll that overlooked another meadow and a line of trees. He pointed vaguely in a northerly direction and said that the Germans were over there. He then added, pointing as he talked, "We have a couple of mortars back there and a machine gun there and there. Let's go back and have another drink."

I thanked our guide very much but told him it was time we returned to our company. Fortunately, the changeover that night went smoothly, and when dawn broke we were in and the British were out.

The next morning, an Italian fellow asked to see me. His name was Gino, and he said that he had been working for the British officers. But now that they were gone, could he work for us? I asked him what exactly he did for the British. His answer was mind-boggling, considering that we were on the front lines in a war zone: "I help with the meals, set the table, serve the food, wash the dishes, and provide the wine."

This sounded too good to be true, so I asked him what it was going to cost. I can't remember the exact figure he quoted, but I do recall that when divided among six officers of our company, it came to less than six bucks a month each. Needless to say, Gino was hired on the spot.

It took a week or two to iron out the rough spots—find a tablecloth, glassware, knives and forks, and the best wine. But, before we knew it, Company M's officer's mess was running in high gear.

A few days later, while taking a walk in "beautiful downtown Bagni de Lucca," I was confronted by our illustrious battalion commander. He demanded to know what the hell was going on in my sector. Rumors of "high living" had reached regimental headquarters. I suggested that he might like to visit our quaint little village, see its impressive small church, and stay for dinner.

The meal was spectacular, but when Gino served him the wine, the look on his face and ensuing comments were well worth the flack I knew I was going to get for the next month or so.

But I'll always be grateful to the British for showing me how to fight a war—circumstances permitting. After all, they had been fighting wars long before the United States fought its first one.

After the German Army surrendered, our battalion was moved from one place to another in northern Italy. Evidently we were to be available in case any of the "natives" became restless.

In July, we returned to the Po Valley to await further orders. But the thought on everyone's mind was, "When are we going home?"

It was about this time that a curious soldier, searching a German warehouse, discovered a cache of French champagne and brandy. Talk about winning the lottery. We had hit the jackpot!

That evening at mess, I was directed to issue a bottle of champagne to the first four men in line, while each fifth soldier would receive a bottle of brandy. It was a typical very warm evening, however, and as soon as a bottle of champagne was opened, most of the bubbly disappeared in foam.

A way had to be found to chill the champagne. I finally solved the problem by having a group of eager soldiers dig a deep hole to serve as a wine cellar.

As officers, we had been issued a small supply of whiskey, and each of us also received a bottle of the brandy. But not all the officers were happy about the way the spoils of war had been distributed. When the wine connoisseurs learned that the champagne was Piper-Heidsieck and Pommery, they had a fit. A frantic barter trade quickly developed—brandy for champagne. Some of the men were tough bargainers.

While waiting for orders to go home, I had a chance to take some R&R. I decided to go to Rome and also visit the Isle of Capri. I had heard that the place to go in Rome was the Hotel Excelsior—especially at the late afternoon cocktail time.

One early evening, when I entered the dining room, I noticed our regimental and battalion commanders, plus several staff officers, seated at a large round table. I walked over to pay my respects and was asked to join them. I was the low-ranking man on the totem pole but figured I might get a free drink or two.

I was really enjoying myself and the table talk when the conversation—as always happens—turned to sex and the current lack of "available women." A colonel, sitting near me, remarked that girls would certainly liven up the party.

I immediately realized that this was my chance to make some points. I had seen several young ladies hanging around the hotel entrance. By this time, I could speak the language well enough to be understood. I asked my newfound drinking buddies to be patient for a few minutes and excused myself from the table.

I hurried outside. The women were still there. I asked the first girl I saw if she could round up about five more gals for drinks and a party. In less than two minutes, I was back at the dining room with a girl on each arm and three more eagerly walking behind me. We were greeted with a standing applause and cheers. Needless to say, I couldn't buy a drink all evening—and a great time was had by all.

My trip to the volcanic Isle of Capri was also a huge success, but in a different sort of way. The town of Capri faced the Bay of Naples and Mount Vesuvius. The island had been turned into an air corps rest center. The infantry and other services were relegated to a small hotel—away from the center of activities—in an area called Anacapri. The hotel faced the Mediterranean and had a good-looking beach. Two large vertical rock formations stood a short distance offshore. The taller of the two was more than a hundred feet high.

The infantrymen were surrounded on all sides by flyboys and continually took a verbal beating. Soldiers who fought the ground war got no respect whatsoever. One evening, while drowning my sorrows with a few new friends, I took a good look at those towers of stone staring at us from across the bay.

It may have been the vino, but suddenly it dawned on me—an infantry flag, flying from the top of the highest rock, would give those air corps types something to think about as to who really won the war.

After a spirited discussion, a brilliant idea was proposed and enthusiastically approved. A chambermaid donated a large white pillowcase and some black cloth. I cut the material into strips resembling the outline of crossed rifles. A seamstress sewed the rifles on each side of the pillowcase.

Another soldier located an iron rod a half-inch in diameter and about ten feet long. We now had our flag and flagpole, and we scrounged up some telephone wire to anchor it to the rock.

The next morning I borrowed a small boat and, with a volunteer, rowed out to the tallest column. The sheer rock wall looked intimidating. But, upon closer examination, the stone face proved to be quite easy to climb. Many cracks and handholds scarred the surface. And, even carrying the flag, iron pole, and wire, I managed to reach the top in half an hour. The cliffs we scaled in Colorado were much more difficult.

I quickly located a suitable crevice and set up the rod and guy wires. Within a few minutes, the army banner was whipping in the strong breeze.

The flag was very noticeable from the island, although the crossed rifles were hard to identify. But with rumorlike speed, everyone on Capri seemed to know who had put up the flag and why. After my return to the States, I was told that the flag kept flying for about three months.

Dan Pinolini, Company I, 86th Mountain Infantry Regiment narrated one of his exciting experiences while on the front lines in Italy.

We had just captured a sector from the Germans that included a farmhouse and stable. While we were digging in and consolidating the position, our platoon commander told me to take a couple of men, go back to regimental headquarters, and retrieve our packs. They had been left there prior to launching the attack.

Since I could speak the language, I was selected to go to the farmhouse and ask if I could borrow a horse and wagon. After a cautious search of the house, I found the farmer and his wife hiding in the basement. After I identified myself as an Italian American, I was greeted like an old friend.

The farmer said he would hitch up two horses to a wagon, but he insisted on driving the team. So while he handled the reins, we relaxed in the back of the wagon. But not for long. German artillery spotters quickly sighted the wagon. We were like targets in a shooting gallery. Shells began exploding on all sides of us. The horses panicked, charged off the road, and raced up a steep hill where they collapsed from exhaustion. We jumped to the ground and dove under the wagon. The farmer didn't wait around. He took off at top speed back to his house.

When the shelling finally stopped, we slipped carefully out from under the wagon. It took us ten minutes to get the horses calmed down and on their feet. I then handled the reins, and it was a wild ride over a rough road to regimental headquarters. After loading the packs on the wagon, I jumped into the driver's seat and we rushed back down the road. We must have looked like cowboys in a western movie as our wagon reached the front trailing a cloud of dust. As soon as they sighted us, the men of our platoon began cheering and clapping like we were heroes. For the rest of the war, I was known as the "Buck Jones of Company I."

"Climb to Glory." The sculpture at Fort Drum, New York, commemorating the 10th Mountain Division's climb up Riva Ridge in February 1945.

Courtesy Major Walter Piatt

Daniel Dean Becker.

Courtesy Daniel Dean Becker

Guardhouse staff, Camp Hale, Colorado. *Front row, left to right:* Patterson, Haliban, Thomas, Peterson, Kinzer. *Back row, left to right:* Bowman, Forney, Zeig, Thompson, Spurgeon, Prison Sergeant Mike Lawlor.

Courtesy Merle G. Forney

Bivouac at the Pisa Staging Area #3.

Courtesy Giancarlo Bendini

Briona, Lake Garda—125th Artillery Battalion shells German position across the lake.

Courtesy Giancarlo Bendini

Gaggio Montano—First Aid Station of the 85th Infantry Regiment on Mount Gorgolesco.

Courtesy Giancarlo Bendini

Vicinetta—Battery B of the 615th Artillery Battalion fires on German positions near Abetone.

Courtesy Giancarlo Bendini

Mount della Torraccia—Engineers search for mines with metal detectors. February 22, 1945.

Courtesy Giancarlo Bendini

Left to right: H. A. Newton, John Minere, and Lloyd Fitch.

Courtesy of Lloyd Fitch

Lieutenant Bob Sabin in front of his dugout near Florence, Italy. April 1945.

Courtesy Robert C. Sabin

Left to right: John Bassett and Woodrow Powers, Company I, 85th Regiment, shown in front of their bunker. April 1945.

Courtesy Robert C. Sabin

After battle, men gulped hungrily at whatever food was available. But even when eating, grimy faces showed watchful tension, and eyes anxiously turned to see where Kraut shells were falling in the town a few hundred yards away. Ears constantly had to listen for the split-second, warning, whining-hiss of incoming rounds to judge their nearness.

Photograph and legend by Richard A. Rocker (1911–1994) 87th U.S. Infantry Regiment

Courtesy Collection of Audrey Wendland

The capture of the strategic road junction town of Castel d'Aiano, and the mountains overlooking it, was the ultimate limited objective of the March 3 attack, successfully completed on March 5. When the job was done, and when the German artillery in its turn had blasted the town and our men in it, the town did not look the same.

Photograph and legend by Richard A. Rocker (1911–1994) 87th U.S. Infantry Regiment

Courtesy Collection of Audrey Wendland

Here is a study of the impact of war upon the individual; this man, photographed right after Pietra Colora and Mount della Croce were taken, had just been relieved after five exceedingly rough and sleepless days and nights. (The fortnight previous was no cinch, either!) His face shows it all, as he rests here beside the quiet guns. This is how most of us looked by then, "the morning after the month before," and it wasn't funny. Only Mauldin could make it look that way. ("Pop" Haus, Co. "I.")

Photograph and legend by Richard A. Rocker (1911–1994) 87th U.S. Infantry Regiment

Courtesy Collection of Audrey Wendland

After too long a time of too many close ones and too little sleep, a smile becomes a twisted grimace and the eyes remember seeing awful things: Raffi Bedayan (Hq. Co., 3 Bn.) can't quite laugh it off.

Photograph and legend by Richard A. Rocker (1911–1994) 87th U.S. Infantry Regiment

Courtesy Collection of Audrey Wendland

Soldiers of Company I, 85th Regiment. *Left to right:* Eugene Srbeng, Francis Penny, John Holman, Gerald Grunwald, and Robert Sabin.

Courtesy Collection of Audrey Wendland

Men of Company I, 85th Regiment, set up a new bivouac near Tora on April 8, 1945. Hill in the background is probably Mount Spicchioni. *Left to right:* Francis Penny, Alfred Latuso, Howard Moore, Bob Sabin, Keith Kvam, and Woodrow Powers.

Photograph by Thomas A. Dreis

Courtesy Collection of Audrey Wendland

Some of the motor pool gang. Company D, 126th Mountain Engineer Battalion. *Front row:* Carver, Rodriguez, Muller, Loshbaugh, Tucker. *Back row:* Barnes, Mackey, Towes, Biernbaum, Lunday.

Courtesy Philip A. Lunday

1st Squad, 1st Platoon, I Company , 87th U.S. Infantry Regiment. April 1945. *Rear row, left to right:* Nichols, Carrico, Manning, Arcado, Acciraito, Steinberg. *Front row, left to right:* Baranowski, O'Millian, Vitalius, Peterson, Kilmer.

Courtesy George W. Peterson

The leaders of I Company, 87th Regiment, 10th Mountain Division. *Left to right:* Top Sergeant Bob Diehl, Lieutenant Russ McJury, Captain Adrian Riordon, Lieutenant Alec Jones. April 14, 1945.

Courtesy George W. Peterson

A German tank knocked out by Company I, 87th Regiment. American soldiers and an Italian civilian are pictured in the photograph.

Courtesy George W. Peterson

Company D, 85th Regiment, 10th Mountain Division, winds its way up the face of Mount Belvedere carrying mortars and ammunition after the enemy had been driven from the heights. February 21, 1945.

A wounded American soldier is evacuated by tramway near Farne, Italy. February 21, 1945.

Sherman tanks in position on the crest of Mount Belvedere after its capture by troops of the 10th Mountain Division. February 23, 1945.

Men of the 110th Signal Company, 10th Mountain Division, stringing communication wires near Carnidello, Italy. April 16, 1945.

Men of the 126th Mountain Engineer Battalion wait for orders to advance toward Tole, Italy, about 300 yards to the front.

German prisoners captured by Company B, 87th Regiment, 10th Mountain Division, are marched to the rear at Tole, Italy. April 1945.

Men of the 85th Regiment, 10th Mountain Division, survey the far bank of the Po River, approximately a mile and a half from San Benedetto. April 24, 1945.

Troops of Company G, Second Battalion, 10th Mountain Division, advance through Verona, Italy. April 26, 1945.

Soldiers of the Second Battalion 85th Regiment move cautiously through Badie, Italy. May 3, 1945.

This BELIEVE IT OR NOT sketch appeared in the June 11, 1945 issue of *The Oregonian.*

Cameron Butte of Company H, 85th Infantry Regiment recalled the incident: "I believe it happened on Hill 409. I don't know the name of the soldier who was killed while on his way to deliver a letter to me. The German soldier who found the letter was a member of an enemy squad on a night patrol.

"Earlier that day, I had posted a machine gun squad a short distance above a foxhole that I was sharing with Conrad Manville. Later that night a member of the machine gun squad sneaked down and alerted us of the approaching enemy. The Germans walked right into our line of fire. I discovered the letter addressed to me on the body of one of the dead Germans."

Courtesy Cameron Butte

Melvin Reiss, Company K, 85th Regiment, sketched this self-portrait on February 4, 1945. On the following day—during a failed attempt to take the town of Pianosinatico—he was shot in the head by a sniper's bullet. Reiss stated, "Heroic teams of medics carried me down the mountain. About twelve hours later, I reached the evacuation hospital, and underwent extensive life-saving surgery."

Mel was not quite nineteen years old when he joined the 10th Mountain Division. He reported to Camp Swift, Texas in July 1944, and was one of the many ski troopers who never learned to ski.

Courtesy Melvin Reiss

V-Mail letter from Glen Dawson to his wife. July 27, 1945.

Courtesy Glen Dawson

CHAPTER 6

The 85th Mountain Infantry Regiment: The Italian Campaign

General Hays planned to employ his entire division—plus artillery, armor, and air power—for an attack on Riva Ridge and Mount Belvedere.

Shortly before midnight on February 18, 1945, four companies of the 86th Mountain Infantry Regiment launched their assault. Armed mainly with rifles and grenades, the ski troops began to climb the cliffs in single file and on parallel routes. Their only light was from flares and an occasional distant shell burst.

Scrambling rapidly over the ridge, the Americans caught the Germans completely by surprise. Savage enemy counterattacks were repeatedly beaten back.

For more than two days, units of the 85th and 86th Regiments—low on supplies and ammunition—held their ground. Army engineers finally managed to erect a tramway to carry men and supplies to the top of the ridge and bring casualties back down to a field hospital.

In his story "The 10th Caught It All at Once," published in the December 8, 1945, issue of the *Saturday Evening Post*, Richard Thruelsen related a remarkable letter written by Private First Class Richard Ryan of Company I, 85th Regiment, and edited here. Ryan vividly described the 10th Mountain's push into the Po Valley:

> The morning of April 14 dawned clear and warm, but the uneasy quiet was soon shattered by our artillery as it began bombarding enemy positions. While waiting for orders to attack, I opened a can of K rations—ham and eggs—and munched on a couple of hard-as-rocks biscuits.
>
> I had barely finished eating when we were on our way into the valley. The air was thick with heavy-clouds of smoke from our support fire. After advancing about two hundred yards, I looked around. The valley was carpeted with men—spread out and moving steadily forward.

Our artillery barrage was still raising smoke ahead of us—when suddenly it stopped. Then I heard the roar of P-47s as they raced in to strafe enemy positions.

We quickly reached the heights. They rose in ridges like a washboard. German artillery had already zeroed-in on every ravine and hiding place we might use. When we reached the top of the second draw, all hell broke loose. Machine gun bullets began zipping overhead. A man in front of me was hit. The frantic shouts of "Medic! Medic!" could be heard above the bedlam.

Our company sneaked around the side of a hill and began shooting at some farmhouses below us. We had been receiving sniper fire from the buildings. Three or four of our men on the forward slope were shot. My platoon leader was hit in both shoulders and a leg, and his runner was mortally wounded. Jim Keck, who teamed up with me in the squad, was struck in the left hip. The bullet deflected off the hip bone, ran up his side, and exited just below the armpit.

Another soldier dashed toward one of the houses. He threw two grenades—killing one of the snipers—before being shot through the head.

We continued our advance—moving rapidly across a couple of open fields. Enemy mortar and artillery fire was heavy. I watched one large shell spinning end over end, screaming its death cry, before hitting the ground about two hundred yards ahead of me.

After what seemed hours of running, creeping, sprawling, and shivering with fear, we finally reached our objective—Hill 913. By this time, it was late in the afternoon. There was a short exchange of hand grenades with enemy troops on the other side of the ridge.

Suddenly, a couple of German soldiers—waving white flags—crawled out from their bunker in a ravine behind us. They were motioned to head toward our rear lines. Surprisingly, they were fired upon by their own men. These same snipers also began working on us. One man after another was picked off—mostly leg wounds.

By nightfall, enemy shelling had slackened. Buck and I were on the nose of the hill and subject to counterattack. We began digging a foxhole but struck stone about two feet down. A couple of wounded soldiers were on the ground near us. One of the men had been shot in both legs, the other in the chest. The medics never showed up, so we carried them down to the first aid station.

At daybreak, the Germans launched a heavy artillery barrage. Shrapnel was zinging everywhere, clipping the bark off trees and branches just above our heads.

It was late in the morning before we dared move to another foxhole farther down the hill. We remained there all day and until the following afternoon when the Germans withdrew.

On the 18th, we were on the move again. The road was choked with dust and smoke as our tanks rumbled past us. I saw a dead American soldier sprawled grotesquely at the side of the road and a German with the top of his head sliced neatly off. We trudged through one village that was completely bombed out and leveled. The stench of death covered the town like a blanket.

Enemy artillery began shelling us. I was exhausted but not hungry. I blacked out for a moment or two while digging in for the night. It was then that I noticed my feet were blistered.

We kept pushing ahead, driving the enemy back. I was in sort of a stupor—very tired and moving like a zombie.

Beyond the next village there was a long stretch of open road, giving the Germans an unobstructed view of any movement. We immediately came under machine gun and sniper fire. Orders were issued to capture the heights ahead. Our tanks lined up and proceeded to saturate the top of the hill with gunfire. An ammunition dump was hit. It exploded in an enormous burst of flame and smoke.

We began advancing across open fields. A shell exploded about twenty-five yards from me. I was thrown to the ground and covered with dirt. I staggered to my feet and kept moving. A dead soldier near the blast was missing a hand.

Tracers began singing over our heads. We hurried through a couple of vineyards then up a hill, halting at the top. I slept in a ditch for a couple of hours—then was on the move again. We soon reached a large villa and dug in near the house.

When morning arrived, my feet hurt—but what a view! Bologna, the Po Valley, and, in the distance, the Alps. It had been six days of bitter fighting against stubbornly defended mountain positions and across extensive minefields.

Early the next morning, the 85th walked out of the Appennines and into the flat terrain of the Po Valley. We had fought our way through eighteen miles of enemy strong points.

With level ground now ahead of us—and where armor and motorized infantry could operate—we began speculating wistfully on the possibility of becoming a rear-echelon outfit. After all, there would be wine cellars to be "secured," pleasant villas to be "liberated," and even time to dry socks and sleep. But this was not to be. General Hays could smell the waters of the Po, and the chase after the retreating enemy would begin immediately.

The order of the day was, "Stick your bayonet in every bush. Nobody knows where the front is!"

As the 10th forged ahead on parallel roads that crossed the valley, the signs of German defeat became more and more apparent. Burned-out trucks, abandoned equipment, and the dead littered the roadsides.

In the sky above us, army Thunderbolts—racing like vengeful messengers of death—bombed and strafed the retreating enemy columns. As the pace of our advance quickened, the character of abandoned vehicles and equipment changed. Most of it now appeared to be in good condition. Surrendering German soldiers emerged from every ditch, house, and barn.

On the morning of April 23, we reached the town of San Benedetto Po. The enemy had so thoroughly destroyed the Po River bridges that not even the skeletal form of a pillar was visible. General Hays decided that we would cross the river in assault boats. The combat engineers had already been cut to pieces attempting to erect a temporary bridge.

As soon as the landing craft were lined up along the shore, the Germans on the opposite bank opened fire with everything they had. One soldier—who had spent five hours in a foxhole with a decapitated friend and 6 mortally wounded signalman—said that shrapnel flooded into the foxhole like a "river of molten metal."

We dug in until the shelling slackened and then ran for the boats. Surprisingly, the actual river crossing went smoothly. But, it was a daring tactical move. For while we were crossing the Po, the division was also attacking the enemy on our right and left flanks.

From the river to the foothills of the Alps, the Germans put up a fight but were kept on the run by our armor and aircraft. As advance units of the 10th Mountain raced north toward Austria, the German Army in Italy surrendered.

German General Fridolin von Senger, commander of the 14th Panzer Corps, declared that the 10th was the best division he had faced on the Russian, Sicilian, or Italian fronts.

Dr. Morton Levitan—a medical officer with the 85th Mountain Infantry Regiment—was captured by the Germans. His story of life as a POW reveals an interesting perspective on the war.

By the time the 10th Mountain Division arrived in Italy, both sides were sick of war and the appalling casualties. Every officer was required to watch a film that, I believe, was titled *San Pietro*. A member of the Salvation Army was the projectionist. Enlisted men were not allowed to view the movie. The reason for this became very plain. As I remember, it included the directions on how to place a body in an evacuation bag—tying the hands together, etc.

My front-line location was a small room in a building that previously had been a tuberculosis sanitarium. The room was bare except for a wash basin with running water and a single light bulb. A machine gun was set up about a hundred feet beyond my window.

On February 21, 1945, I was on a hill observing the action with Colonel Raymond Barlow. He told me to go find Lieutenant Colonel John Stone, commanding the Second Battalion, and tell him to continue his attack until the battalion was expended.

I assumed that Barlow wanted to impress Stone by having me deliver the orders instead of sending a runner. I had never met Stone and gave the message to Red MacIntyre, who said he would take care of it.

The following day, I heard that there were several wounded men on the hill. And since no patients were in the aid station, I decided to go up and come back with the litter bearers. I had no sooner climbed the hill than I came upon two soldiers who were crouched below a small rise. They were waiting for orders to make a dash across an open area that was exposed to sniper fire. They had been instructed to cross the field at different intervals, each soldier watching where the other had made his run.

Suddenly, however, I was called back to check one of the wounded men. By the time I returned to the slope, the two soldiers had already left.

Without thinking of the danger, I crept over the hillock but then followed a path that ran across the north slope of Mount Gorgolesco. I should have realized that I was moving in the wrong direction when suddenly I came under sniper fire. Bullets ricocheted off the rocks around me. I began to run. This wasn't the time to stop and ask directions.

Moments later, a German soldier blocked my path. We looked at each other in surprise. But since I wasn't armed, he didn't shoot me. The soldier demanded, "Was wollen Sie?" (What do you want?) I answered him in German, "Ich bin Arzt." (I am a physician.)

The soldier motioned me to follow him and asked, "Haben sie Waffen?" (Do you have weapons?) I answered in the negative, and he marched me down a narrow trail to a dugout.

The dugout was remarkably well constructed and even had red polka-dot curtains on the windows. As I entered the shelter, I noticed one man snoring away on a top bunk. My captor introduced me to a young officer who couldn't have been more than twenty years old.

Both Germans were anxious to hear my story, but before I had a chance to catch my breath, the officer asked me if I knew who was responsible for the war. Caught unawares, I replied, "No, who?!" He answered it was the Jews. I then informed him that I was a Jew. He smiled benignly at me—assuming that I had misunderstood him—and corrected me. "No, I didn't mean that you were a Jew. I meant that the Jews were responsible for the war."

I told him that I understood exactly what he said. The conversation stopped right there, giving me a chance to survey my surroundings and have a smoke. But, when I opened my first aid kit to get a pack of cigarettes, I discovered that I had taken the kit belonging to the BSA—battalion surgeon assistant. In this case, however, the initials stood for "Bull Shit Artist!"

I remember the time that I asked him why he decided to become an army medical officer. His answer was that he felt he was too good to be an enlisted man. I later heard that our regimental surgeon pulled him off the front lines because he was as useless as balls on a brass monkey. As soon as the shells started to fall, he crawled under the nearest table.

But, to continue my story, I decided to check the surgeon assistant's first aid kit. As luck would have it, however, there were no cigarettes or whiskey in the kit. (I always managed to pack a bottle of government-issued booze for "first aid" purposes.)

Instead, the bag was half full of condoms, packed in cellophane and arranged in neat rows of a dozen each. Fortunately, the kit also contained some medical supplies—several morphine syringes.

The Germans immediately confiscated the first aid kit. Later, a soldier from a different division traded some of the condoms for apples.

Meanwhile, I had time to study my captors. The soldier who took me prisoner was middle-aged—probably forty years old. I believe a younger German would have shot me.

I couldn't help liking the young officer and decided to engage him in conversation. I inquired about his profession in civilian life. He seemed surprised that I asked the question and said that he was an engineer. I then asked that since I was a noncombatant, could I return to my medical unit? I knew it was a stupid question but figured there was no harm in asking. He shook his head negatively and looked at me in disbelief that I would even make such a request.

A few minutes later, the officer received a phone message with instructions on what to do with his prisoner. A soldier was assigned to take me to headquarters for interrogation. We had barely left the dugout when the officer ran after us and pushed a few packages of food into my arms. He said, "Take it! Take it! You'll need it!" He then ran back to the dugout without giving me a chance to thank him.

I was escorted down a path toward a village below Mount Gorgo-lesco. The road was being continually strafed by American planes, so we crept along the hillside of the trail while trying to be as inconspicuous as possible.

We came upon the bodies of three Germans lying in the middle of the path. The men were obviously dead, but my guard motioned me to check them. So, I held the wrist of each soldier—as if hunting for a pulse—while, at the same time, looking skyward for any aircraft.

Upon reaching the village, I was taken to a store that was being used as a first aid station. While there, I saw one German soldier come in for treatment. He was definitely goldbricking. A medic hurriedly ran a flashlight over him, then told the fellow that there was nothing wrong with him.

I had a short conversation with the medic during which I tried to teach him how to pronounce "penicillin" correctly. While being a prisoner, I always strived to direct any conversation toward medical subjects and to bring the German doctors up to date on the latest advances of medicine.

I was soon put in a room behind the store where several civilians were huddled together. They were overjoyed to see me and believed I had brought them luck since the village had not been shelled that day. But, moments later, American artillery opened fire, and close by explosions shook the store. Women and children began screaming. This was the first time I was afraid—very afraid. I don't know how to explain it except that the screaming and shell explosions touched off all the tensions that had been building up inside of me.

An elderly Italian woman brought me a bowl of soup, offering it to me with both hands and a warm smile. She looked me directly in the eyes as if to say, "Don't be afraid. Everything will be all right."

Two German soldiers were assigned to take me to the next village, where the commanding major was stationed. These two soldiers were from Yugoslavia and spoke both Slavic and German. Whenever they conversed in their native language, I couldn't understand a word they said.

During the march, I kept thinking of items I had with me that I didn't want to fall into enemy hands. As we crossed a small bridge, I asked to relieve myself. While doing my duty, I emptied my pockets of everything into a fast-flowing stream. The soldiers may have noticed, but it was too late to do anything about it, so they just nudged me to keep moving.

I wondered why I was being escorted by two men. My guess is that guerrillas were operating in the vicinity. From time to time, I would hear a whistle. One of my guards would quickly answer the signal. Evidently, this was a challenge and password.

When we reached the village, I was invited to have dinner with the major and his young staff officer. I could tell that the young man was bristling at the thought that he was sitting at the same table with a Jew.

The major was older—very correct and congenial. He offered me a drink of schnapps, which I gratefully accepted. I regretfully declined a second drink—although it was excellent schnapps. The major smiled, understanding my position as a prisoner of war.

It was an enjoyable dinner with pleasant conversation. The major only asked me two questions that were out of line. I can't remember exactly how he worded the first, but he obviously wanted to know if his men were surrendering. I hesitated to answer but then truthfully said that I had not seen many German dead.

My host seemed a little irritated at my reply, then asked where I got my southern German accent. I was surprised at the question, since I was only required to give my name, rank, and serial number. I satisfied his curiosity by telling him that I had studied in Switzerland.

Our meal was suddenly interrupted by the arrival of the commanding general. The major attempted to introduce me, but the general hurried past us and without turning his head, asked, "Was wollen Sie von armen dem Deutchland?" (What do you want of the poor Germany?) I answered with a forced laugh and shrug.

A few minutes later, I was ordered into a small car and taken to some sort of prison. I was hustled into a large barracks room filled with rows of cots where German soldiers were sleeping, smoking, or talking in low voices so as not to awaken their comrades.

I sat on a cot for several minutes, wondering what was going to happen to me. I didn't have long to wait. An officer sat down next to me and immediately began denigrating the Americans. He vehemently claimed that we used litter bearers to carry weapons and ammunition. As I listened to his tirade, I noticed that the other soldiers in the room had stopped talking.

By this time, I was very tired and in no mood to listen to his continual harangue. I answered him in German, "Dieser Fall ist wahrscheinlich passiert. Mehrmals. Auf beiden Seiten. Was wollen Sie, einen gemuetlichen Krieg?" (This case has probably happened. Several times. On both sides. What do you want, a cozy war?)

The officer was shocked at my answer. He sat there a few moments without saying a word, then stood up and walked away. I could sense the tension filling the room, the men silent—listening to the officer—and anxiously waiting for his reply that never came.

A couple of guards soon showed up and took me to a cell on the top floor of the building. I tried to read some writing that had been scratched into a wall—probably by other prisoners—but exhaustion got the best of me, and I passed out.

It seemed that I had barely fallen asleep when I was awakened by the sounds of an air raid. I was quickly hustled into the basement. The guard wore a German uniform but had Asian features. I tried to converse with him, but he didn't speak German. I later learned that he was a soldier who had been taken prisoner on the Russian front and had volunteered to serve in the German Army. I was told that there were three German divisions composed of these ex-prisoners.

I also met another Russian wearing a German uniform. He said that after being sent to Italy, he refused to fight for the Germans and was to be sent back to Germany. I asked what would happen to him. He answered with a prophetic shrug, "They'll shoot me!"

One afternoon, I was escorted to a private house to examine and treat a couple of wounded Americans. Their guards were older men. I remember one of the Germans spoke to me in Italian.

The next stop on my journey was a brick school building where I was put in a small room with a guard outside the door. In the middle of the night, an aircraft flew over and dropped a bomb that exploded outside my window. The sound of the blast—plus steel fragments shredding the glass and thin wooden blinds—was terrifying. Luckily, I was sleeping on a straw mat in one corner of the room. The hot shrapnel plowed into the wall just above my head.

The mood of the officers here was bitter. It seems that the farther to the rear I went, the more antagonistic the Germans became. This was just the exact opposite for enemy soldiers taken prisoner by the Americans. The farther they were brought behind our lines, the better their treatment.

I asked one of the officers if I could borrow a razor to shave. Another overheard my remark and answered, "Let him cut his throat!" This officer was particularly angry, blaming the Americans for his being in the army. He was a lawyer in civilian life and had only recently been called up to serve his country.

After being cooped up for a few days, I was brought outside with a few other prisoners to sit in the sun. In the distance, we watched several American planes dive-bombing a target. There was no opposition, but the last plane in line did not dive as deep as the aircraft ahead of it.

We began laughing at the chicken pilot, but our guard did not appreciate the humor and ordered us back inside the building. I tried to explain to the German soldier that the same rivalry existed between our air force and infantry as it did in every army and that we were only laughing at the pilot who did not dive as deep as the others. I lost the argument, however, and remained penned up.

At our next stop we were joined by a few American prisoners from another division. I sensed a certain resentment among these men and wondered if they blamed their officers for having been captured.

That evening—like they were feeding a pack of dogs—a guard threw us a few loaves of bread and some sausage. The prisoners pounced on the food like wild animals. I stopped the scuffle and told the men that we were going to divide the rations like civilized people.

I told a sergeant—the ranking noncom—to slice the bread and sausage as evenly as possible. Then, after the enlisted men had been fed, I kept the last piece for myself. In this way, I was able to maintain some control over the prisoners.

While imprisoned here, I was called out a few times by some SS officers—mainly because they didn't have anything else to do. They would ask a couple of questions and then proceed to talk about themselves. I quickly became a good listener, since there were always American cigarettes on the table.

I remember one SS officer who showed me his notebook of propaganda leaflets. These flyers would be shot over our lines in a shell that would explode and scatter the contents. He was quite proud of them and asked my opinion. I studied his works of art carefully, mulling over my reply. After a couple of minutes, I told the officer that they were very well done and could incite men to revolt. But, since we were winning the war, they did not have that result. He agreed with me and said that one officer gathered up the leaflets and nailed them to a latrine wall. With his works of art being treated so sacrilegiously, the poor guy was practically in tears. So, I just pocketed a pack of cigarettes on the table and walked out of the room.

At this stage of the war, the Germans were taking very few prisoners, so they moved us around to keep ahead of the advancing Americans. Our guards would pack us into trucks, place a board across the back, and have the POWs face the rear. We always moved at night. I noticed that the rear wheels of the truck behind us were way out of line. There was no maintenance of equipment. The Germans didn't seem to care.

One time when we stopped, the guards lit their pipes. The glow from the match flames could be seen for miles. An American soldier could never have gotten away with that trick.

I often wondered why the Germans kept on fighting in Italy after the Italians surrendered. I did overhear a couple of our guards talking about a secret weapon that Hitler was supposed to have, but the tone of their voices was not very optimistic.

At one of our stops, we were hustled into the basement room of a large building and were joined by ten more American prisoners. Among the POWs was an officer, Sylvester Decker. He had received a field commission but told me that accepting the officer rank was a mistake. He felt more comfortable as a sergeant.

I had my closest call with death here when an angry German officer called me out of the room. He marched me down a hallway, around a corner, and down another hall. As soon as we were out of hearing range from the other prisoners, he began chastising me. He was very bitter and all worked up over the Allied bombing of Dresden.

I tried to calm the officer down and told him that since my capture, I had heard nothing about the air raid. But, that didn't seem to satisfy him. His fury increased as he continued the tirade. Then, with his spittle flying in my face, he remarked, "It would do you Americans good to know what it's like to be bombed!" I nodded my agreement and answered, "You're right!"

The German drew back and seemed surprised that I agreed with him. He evidently decided that my reply was so spontaneous that it must have been an honest answer, and his verbal attack subsided. It was then that I noticed he was holding a revolver in his right hand. He put the pistol away, turned slowly around, and walked down the hall. With a nervous sigh of relief, I hurried back to the relative safety of my fellow POWs.

Another dangerous incident occurred as the Germans prepared to move us from this location. One of the prisoners was wearing a sharpshooter's badge. A guard noticed the badge and assumed that the soldier was a sniper. The boy's name was Hadley. He was a tall, gangling fellow from Kentucky—very friendly and always smiling.

As we lined up in formation ready to climb in the trucks, a German officer and this guard moved in behind Hadley and ordered him to the front of the line. The officer then demanded Hadley's dog tags. We were surprised at the order. All the prisoners knew they were not to give them up.

As the officer grabbed the dog-tag chain, Hadley resisted. A dangerous situation quickly developed. I whispered to Hadley that it was okay to surrender the tags, and he reluctantly handed them over. One of the German guards began snickering, which did not improve the already tense situation.

I later talked to another sergeant about the dog tags. He must have known the officer, because he retrieved the tags and returned them to Hadley.

The next day, all the POWs were crammed into canvas-covered trucks and warned that anyone sneaking a peek under the canvas would be shot. A Russian prisoner with our group asked me to translate. When I told him what we had been warned not to do, he took out a small hidden penknife and cut a peephole in the covering.

Our convoy soon reached a ferryboat landing at the Po River, but the ferry could only carry one truck at a time. A funny episode happened here. The boat captain and the convoy commander carried on a furious argument. The skipper of the ferry said that his orders were that all prisoners must disembark from the vehicles during the river crossing.

The German officer in charge of the prisoners angrily claimed he had orders that the POWs were to remain on the trucks. While this ranting and raving was going on, a small, stout, middle-aged German—wearing a raincoat that came down to his ankles—was continually jabbering about his wife. It was "meine Frau" this and "meine Frau" that. With all three conversations blending together, I had the impression that his frau was going to decide whether we climbed off the trucks or not. The heated discussion finally ended, and we remained aboard the vehicles.

After crossing the Po, we were taken to a POW camp and joined a couple of hundred other prisoners of different nationalities. The French soldiers were kept in two separate groups—those who were captured early in the war, and the others after France surrendered.

An information network operated within the compound. Every day, an Italian dentist came into camp, his instruments wrapped in a daily newspaper. That's how we kept in touch with the outside world. The Germans never did catch on. They thought we had a secret radio hidden somewhere in the camp.

On the day President Franklin D. Roosevelt died (April 12, 1945), all the POWs were assembled and the president's death was announced with great fanfare over loudspeakers. Of course, we had already read the news—courtesy of the dentist.

Word was passed throughout the camp to be deadpan and not show any emotion. The German commandant thought we had misunderstood his remarks and repeated them a second time. The reaction was the same, stonelike faces showing no emotion whatsoever. Just before the mike was cut off, the angry voice of the commandant could be heard accusing us of having a radio.

On April 15, we were packed into railroad boxcars for a hurried trip to Germany. Most of the train tracks had been destroyed by Allied bombing raids. The POWs were taken off the train twice and climbed aboard trucks to continue the journey.

The first time, we sat on boards across the back of the vehicle with a canvas curtain separating us from a load of German bread. Two French-Canadian officers were the bravest men in our group. They managed to move the canvas cover without being seen and grabbed a few loaves, which they shared with the rest of us.

We were loaded into the second truck differently. All the officers, including myself, were ordered to climb in first and told to sit down with our backs against the cab of the vehicle. A German soldier then had us sit cross-legged before sending in the next row. Each group of POWs was arranged in the same manner.

As soon as the truck was full, the convoy commander warned the POWs that any prisoner who stood up would be shot. Everyone was cramped and could barely move. Little by little the men in the front row pushed back to get more leg room. The other rows did likewise. My row was squeezed to the point where I couldn't put up with it anymore.

I stood up, making some remark that one of the prisoners misinterpreted. He started to laugh. Then I did say something funny, and everybody began laughing. The guard didn't know what was going on. He sat there bug-eyed. He had orders to shoot, but when all the POWs began standing up and joking around, the guard just sat there confused.

We soon entered the foothills of the Alps. My memory for details fails here, but I do remember the prison camp guard who told me that there was no point in my filling out a Red Cross POW form, as nothing was getting through the Brenner Pass. So, I didn't fill it out, and my family didn't learn I was still alive until the end of the war.

Glen Dawson related his experiences with the 85th Mountain Infantry Regiment at Camp Swift, Texas, and while serving with the regiment's headquarters company.

I was in the third platoon of Company I, 85th Regiment, 10th Mountain Division at Camp Swift, Texas. I had the rank of T/5—Technician Fifth Grade, equivalent to a corporal. There was really no place for a T/5 in an infantry company, but I was made assistant squad leader.

The company sergeants were regular army soldiers who probably never graduated high school, and most likely had spent much of their service in Hawaii. They had no use for mountains. We called them "pineapple boys."

I remember the day a new man was assigned to my squad. The next morning we turned out for an important inspection. As the colonel strode past us, he took a good look at the new fellow then turned to our company commander and critically remarked, "That man didn't shave!"

As a result, the platoon sergeant and I were confined to the base for the weekend, while the unshaven soldier wasn't penalized. I was learning real fast how the army works.

This man who caused me to lose my weekend pass was also absent when gas masks were handed out. I asked the company quartermaster for an extra one but was told that the masks were in short supply and no more were available. I explained the situation to my platoon sergeant. His sarcastic reply was, "Go find one!"

I pondered the problem for a minute or two, realizing that it was against all my training and ethics to steal. But then suddenly I had a brilliant idea—if I could pull it off. As soon as the sergeant left the barracks, I grabbed his mask and gave the young recruit mine. Every man in my squad now had the required gas masks—except, of course, the sergeant.

Early the next morning, we were rousted out for another inspection. It was still dark when the bugler played reveille. The lights came on. We scrambled to get dressed, grabbed our equipment, and lined up in formation outside the barracks. The sergeant arrived late, but without his gas mask. He was boiling mad and didn't talk or look at me. He knew what had happened, and two days later I was transferred to headquarters company. After we left Camp Swift, I still had to carry a rifle—but didn't have to carry a gas mask.

While in Italy, I was a clerk for Major Kober, the regiment's intelligence officer. Most of the time, I was assigned to the night shift—often quiet, but occasionally very active.

We usually set up headquarters in a large building, home, or villa. Attached to our unit was a three-man POW interrogation team consisting of an officer, a guard, and Jerry Liberman—also a T/5. Jerry was Jewish—fluent in German and also able to communicate in Italian.

Jerry was a good cook, and we often ate together rather than at the company mess. German prisoners were processed by the team, and whenever the interrogators found a compatible worker or cook, the man would be kept at headquarters as long as possible before being sent to the rear.

Jerry had his own personal jeep and fitted it out with comfortable, non-GI padded seats. During lulls in the action, we would use the jeep to take sight-seeing trips. Jerry was a fast, reckless driver, and I had a difficult time trying to slow him down.

I remember one morning after several days of snow and rain, we jumped in the jeep and headed out into the Italian countryside. We hurried past fast-flowing streams and raced down narrow village streets that were perched perilously on the sides of hills. Snow-covered mountain peaks loomed above us as we dashed by terraced vineyards and flocks of grazing goats.

All of a sudden, we found the road blocked by a landside. But this impediment didn't bother us. Jerry locked up the jeep, and we began walking down a stone-lined trail that ran along the side of a steep cliff.

We soon came to a small, charming village with palms, conifers, and gardens. The houses had designs painted on the fronts. Although the shops were closed, there was an air of festivity as uniformed soldiers of different nationalities paraded through the streets.

On another occasion, we accidently came upon one of our outposts. The soldiers were surprised and wanted to know who we were and what we were doing there. It seems we had driven up to a frontline position.

Jerry had painted a large German regimental insignia on the side of his jeep and spoke better German than English, so we probably wouldn't have fared too badly if we had kept on going instead of stopping at the outpost.

The closest I came to the real fighting was at Mount Belvedere. We climbed a steep muddy trail and soon reached a hillside farmhouse. Several large, smelly oxen were billeted on the ground floor.

We remained here overnight. There was much coming and going— fresh troops going up, and the wounded coming down. At times, the front lines would be static for several days, and observation posts were set up near the tops of ridges.

The Germans had their own observation sites on mountains to the north. The terrain in between was usually a no-man's-land dotted with houses. It was easy to tell who was occupying a dwelling by the amount of smoke rising from the chimney. A slight smudge revealed an Italian family, while a somewhat larger amount was evidence that the Germans had taken up residence. But if there was a lot of smoke, it was the Americans burning up fuel like there was no tomorrow.

One of my jobs was to record reports of enemy activity phoned into headquarters. Each observation post seemed to have its own line. Tangled wires were all over the place. Most of the time, I was the person who talked to the soldiers manning the forward positions.

The front lines were fluid as we entered the Po Valley, with some units racing ahead and leaving pockets of the enemy behind. Our troops confiscated German vehicles, civilian trucks, and automobiles—along with gasoline to run them. All of a sudden, the 10th Mountain became a motorized division.

I was with a truck convoy at one time, waiting for orders to move north, when a German soldier on a motorcycle attempted to break through our lines. The poor fellow was immediately shot dead. I thought he could have been stopped and captured—but war isn't a pleasant business.

The night after we crossed the Po River, regimental headquarters took over a farmhouse. The dwelling was overcrowded with frightened civilians, so I scouted around for a more quiet billet.

On the banks of a nearby dike, I stumbled across an abandoned enemy dugout. It had been recently built with new lumber, and the floor was covered with fresh straw. There were sleeping quarters for two men plus a living area. Another soldier and I spent a comfortable night there, with ten feet of hard ground above us as protection from enemy shells.

After we reached Lake Garda, headquarters commandeered a magnificent two-story pink-stucco villa. It was surrounded by beautiful gardens and had a commanding view of the lake. The only inconvenience I can recall is that there was no electricity and the plumbing didn't work.

There were times when we moved our location every day and I did not have the luxury of an Italian villa. One night, when the headquarters billet was full, I found a nearby cemetery with an elaborate vacant brick and concrete crypt. It was a well-protected sleeping room—but the bed was very hard.

Some of the soldiers rigged up elaborate alarm systems using wires and tin cans, so that anyone approaching our headquarters would be heard. On another occasion, when we set up in an open area, I slept in a shallow ditch that had been dug by a soldier who had moved out just before we arrived.

A sheet of corrugated iron covered the foxhole and served as one of the simplest types of dugouts. The men built shelters out of anything and everything—dirt, logs, boards, shell cases, tin cans, and whatever else was at hand.

On May 2, 1945, we received word that the German Army in Italy had surrendered. Some of our soldiers celebrated the news by firing their rifles and machine guns into the air. This was probably the most dangerous fifteen minutes of my army career.

I heard that several high-ranking officers traveled by boat to Mussolini's summer home and looted the place. The line between stealing and "to the victor belong the spoils" is very thin and indefinite.

Now that the war in Italy was over, I took some long walks—alone and unarmed. There was an enormous amount of stonework everywhere—along the narrow streets, walls, and embankments. There were also many vineyards and impressive views of the mountains and lakes.

About this time, the Allies were concerned that Yugoslavian troops commanded by Marshall Tito might attempt to occupy parts of Italy. So, in late May, the 85th Regiment was ordered to Tarcento even though some of Tito's men were stationed there.

Our headquarters company had first choice of location and picked a large five-story stone castle with broad staircases, magnificent statuary, and an imposing view that overlooked the town.

From here, I was transferred to an old hotel in Austria that was next to a glacier and the Gross Glockner. An alpine teaching program was planned but was soon terminated. I returned to the States, presumably to prepare for the invasion of Japan. But as our ship steamed into New York Harbor, we learned that the war in the Pacific had ended, and my army career came to an abrupt and welcome conclusion.

H. Sewall Williams from Stowe, Vermont, related a different kind of war story while serving with Company H, 85th Mountain Infantry Regiment.

As I remember, it was a bitter cold day in February 1945. I was in command of a mortar platoon, and we were struggling up a rugged slope in the Apennine Mountains. During the climb, I noticed an Italian partisan leading a mule train up the steep incline. The animals were loaded down with weapons, ammunition, and reels of wire. The young Alpini in charge of the pack-train was wearing a distinctive peaked green hat. It had a red and white emblem sewn on one side and was decorated with a rumpled feather.

As I watched the partisan urging the animals forward, I saw that he had a firm grip on the tail of one of the mules to help pull him up the slope.

Suddenly, I had a bright idea. I speak terrible Italian but managed to make myself understood to the Alpini. I offered to trade the cigarettes and candy in my K rations for his jaunty hat and a grip on the animal's tail. With a big smile on his face, the Alpini handed me the hat and the tail of the mule.

I put the hat in my backpack, preferring the protection of a steel helmet. After all, you can never tell when a German sniper might be in the neighborhood.

As I tightened my grip on the mule's tail, I shouted "giddyap!" but the animal refused to move. I tried other words—still no luck. My exasperation finally got the best of me, and I grudgingly handed the tail back to the partisan. He was grinning from ear to ear as the stubborn beast quickly became lively and, to my chagrin, both man and mule moved effortlessly up the slope.

However, I still had the hat, and carried it through the battles for Mount della Spe and the spring offensive.

I was also a photography buff during the war and carried my 35mm camera with me everywhere. Although it was against army regulations for unauthorized persons to take photographs, I felt it was okay since my mortar crew was always behind a mountain ridge or slope. If ordered to retreat from our position, I knew that I would have plenty of time to destroy the camera and film.

Fortunately, my unit was never ordered to withdraw. So, by the time hostilities ended in May 1945, I had fifteen rolls of exposed film in my pack.

Later that month, I managed to get a one-day pass to Venice. I hailed a gondola to take me to St. Mark's Square, and that's where I met Lieutenant Sydney Skinner—a British officer from Yorkshire, England.

After an interesting cruise along the canals, Sydney invited me—only a staff sergeant—to the officer's club for a drink. During our conversation, I told Sydney about my rolls of film and how important the pictures were to me. I also remarked that I was afraid the films would be confiscated when I boarded a troopship for the voyage home.

It was then my new friend stated that he was in the signal corps and had access to a darkroom. Sydney offered to develop the pictures and mail them to me.

I never had any doubt that Sydney would keep his word, but that's when fate intervened. I had no sooner returned to camp than I became ill and ran a high fever. I was rushed by ambulance to the nearest tent hospital. A spinal tap revealed I had polio, and within a few days I was paralyzed from the waist down. I was flown to Miami, Florida, and taken to a regional hospital where I underwent physical therapy.

I had been there only a couple of weeks when one of the therapists remarked that an inquiry had been made concerning a sergeant by the name of Harold S. Williams. That was my official name on the army's records, but everyone knew me as Sewall Williams—an old family name.

However, before I could check into the matter, I was transferred to a hospital in Atlantic City, New Jersey. This move was at the request of my uncle, Walter Edge, governor of the state.

A few months later while I was sitting in my wheelchair on the boardwalk, a tightly wrapped brown paper package was delivered to me. It was from Lieutenant Skinner. Sydney had finally found me.

I later learned that the package of pictures had been returned to him several times. He finally appealed to the adjutant general, and this time his persistence paid off.

I couldn't thank Sydney enough for going to all this trouble for a person he had only met once, and we corresponded for many years. Some of the photographs were enlarged and now decorate the walls of the U.S. Army Warfare School in Jericho, Vermont. Many others have appeared in numerous articles and books.

Fortunately, after returning home to Vermont, I regained the use of my legs and started to ski again. And, of course, I still take pictures every chance I get.

Shortly after the end of World War II, Sewall Williams opened a ski lodge near Mad River, Vermont.

Marty Daneman, Headquarters, Second Battalion, 85th Mountain Infantry Regiment, related a unique experience during a chance encounter while on a brief respite from the fighting.

On March 21, 1945, my battalion was pulled out of the front lines and trucked to the Italian resort town of Montecatini for a few days of rest and relaxation. We were filthy dirty, exhausted, and still reeling from the bloody battles and heavy casualties suffered during our attacks on Mount della Torraccia, and the peaks adjacent to Mount della Spe.

The town of Montecatini was infested with ladies of pleasure. And, for most of the men, taking off their rucksacks was the second thing they did after jumping off the trucks. But that didn't appeal to me. My first priority was a hot shower and a clean uniform. Then came party time.

A few blocks from our hotel was a large and busy nightclub. It offered a continuous floor show featuring local talent and, of course, wine, champagne, and grappa brandy.

I hooked up with Dave, a new replacement in my squad. We parked ourselves at a ringside table and proceeded to wash our troubles away. It only took us about an hour to polish off a couple of bottles of grappa, and by this time we were pretty well soused. Dave was in worse shape than me, so I decided to take him back to the hotel while I could still remember where it was.

It didn't take me long, however, to discover that carrying Dave was going to be a problem. I was a thin, wiry fellow, only five and a half feet tall, while my pal was a 200-pound six-footer. It was difficult, but I finally managed to drag Dave outside into the cold night. I laid his limp body on the curb and sat down next to him.

I realized that this was as far as I was going to get hauling Dave's heavy frame around. The street was very dark, and while I was wondering what to do next, a jeep came rumbling down the cobblestone road. The driver was alone; his helmet identified him as a GI. I hailed the driver to stop and explained that my buddy was ill and that I needed help to get him back to our hotel.

Without saying a word, the soldier got out of his vehicle and helped me dump Dave into the back seat. I pointed the way to the hotel, and minutes later we pulled up in front.

The stranger helped me haul my buddy out of the jeep and draped him across my shoulder. I mumbled my eternal gratitude. But then, just as I turned to enter the building, the shielded light above the entrance revealed the identity of the driver. He wore the silver eagles of a colonel and the cross of a chaplain. He never uttered a word of criticism. Perhaps he just understood.

John Hawkins, Company M, 85th Mountain Infantry Regiment, related several interesting comments regarding his service with the 10th Mountain Division.

Before joining the army in the spring of 1943, I was a member of the University of Nevada ski team. In the middle of basic training, I was sent to Camp Hale, Colorado, where the 10th Mountain was being formed. I was immediately attached to a recon unit that included many of the foremost skiers and mountaineers in the country.

In October 1943, I became a member of a group assigned to instruct the troops in rock climbing at Seneca Rock, West Virginia. One of our officers was Lieutenant Dave Bower. After the war, he headed the Sierra Club and was an outstanding advocate for protecting America's natural resources.

After a year of teaching rock climbing, I returned to the 10th Mountain and was assigned to Company M, 85th Mountain Infantry Regiment. The company commander was Kenneth England, an All-American basketball player at the University of Kentucky.

Our company went overseas on the *West Point*. We landed at Naples, Italy, and moved north to the front.

Concerning my combat experiences, I was never sure where I was, why I was there, or what we were trying to accomplish. Our first major assignment was to capture Mount Belvedere. The heights overlooked the road to Bologna. It was a night operation, and we were under constant small arms and mortar fire.

I was later wounded and taken to an aid station. But it had been mined, and I was blown out of the building. I was fortunate to live through the explosion; however, many men did not survive the blast.

Upon my return to duty, I was attached to Company I of the 85th. One of our officers was Robert Dole, later a U.S. senator. I remained with the company until the end of the war. I believe we lost about forty-three men killed and at least twice that number wounded.

One would think that when the war in Italy was over the loss of lives would also end, but such was not the case. A few days after the armistice, several of us were being schooled in the proper use of a Browning automatic rifle (BAR).

We were grouped in a circle around the instructor when I suddenly realized that I was looking down the business end of the BAR. Having been around guns all of my life, I wasn't comfortable sitting in front of a gun barrel, so I moved behind the teacher. Moments later, he placed an ammo clip in the weapon and the gun fired, killing the man where I had been sitting and wounding the soldiers on either side of him.

Although our basic training seemed satisfactory, we were still not prepared for actual combat. I observed one company that came under artillery fire when it entered a heavily wooded area. Shrapnel from shell bursts in the treetops killed and wounded a number of men. In other European sectors, our troops had been instructed to hug the trees when they came under this kind of attack. But we were never told about this tactic.

I have my own resentments regarding the Italian campaign. The first is Winston Churchill's insistence that the Allies open up a front in Italy. All the advantages were with the Germans. They commanded the heights, and the terrain was perfect for defensive warfare.

Another complaint is General Mark Clark's plan to cut off the Germans south of Rome. He wanted to be commander of the first American unit to enter the city. But this pause in the offensive permitted the enemy to escape and set up defensive positions in the north. So much for a general's ego. The Italian campaign could have been ended south of Rome. Anytime a commanding officer's self-interest replaces the concern for his men, I question his ability to lead.

Jay Charles, First Scout, Second Platoon, Company C, 85th Mountain Infantry Regiment, recalled a few interesting experiences, including meeting President Harry Truman.

I was part of a detail assigned to ride atop tanks. Late one afternoon as we rounded a mountain, we sighted a column of German soldiers about a thousand yards below us. Everyone opened fire at once. When the shooting stopped, I asked a lieutenant next to me if I could go down and try to get the Germans to surrender. He told me to go ahead.

As I approached the enemy, I noticed many dead and wounded. I held my rifle above my head and shouted in German, "Don't shoot, American!" A German officer and his company cautiously came out from a wooded area. The officer had seen me give one of his wounded men my extra battle bandage and was very appreciative.

I marched the Germans toward our lines, but about a hundred yards from the tanks enemy artillery opened fire on the mountain road. I yelled to the prisoners, "Get to the tanks!" Everybody jumped aboard, and we hurriedly left the area.

About evening, we arrived at a village. The prisoners were moved into a secure enclosure where they were questioned by our officers. The next day, I was back riding on a tank—beats walking!

After crossing the Po, we stopped in the vicinity of the Villa Franca airport. There was no cover—only a few scattered trees. Just before dark, I heard an aircraft motor. The plane was coming in from the north. Suddenly, I noticed little green dots in the sky arching toward us like a line of fireworks, but without any sound.

I stopped for a moment, mesmerized by the flashing lights. Then it hit me. They were tracers. The aircraft went into a dive, the green dots heading straight for us. I ran like a bat out of hell shouting to my squad, "Take cover!" Machine gun bullets stitched a seam in the earth as the plane pulled up and sped away.

The enemy air attack was over in seconds. I had been surprised by the green tracers. Up to this time, I had only seen orange and red colors. But this was one lesson you only learn once. The airfield was soon captured, and we never saw that German again.

Meeting President Harry Truman was one of the high points of my life. It was in May 1952. I was a New York City motorcycle police officer at the time when our command received orders to escort President Truman and his staff from LaGuardia Airport to the United Nations.

I was one of eleven officers assigned to the escort detail. It was an impressive sight as the president's plane landed and taxied to the disembarkation area. A U.S. Marine honor guard snapped to attention, and the band struck up "Hail to the Chief."

President Truman greeted the awaiting dignitaries and waved to us and the crowd of bystanders as he entered one of four large limousines. His staff filled the other three automobiles. Upon a signal from our lieutenant, we kick-started our motors, switched on the red warning lights, and with sirens screaming escorted the president's convoy to the United Nations.

Then, at President Truman's request, we were invited to have lunch at the UN commissary, after which we were ordered, "Mount up!" But, just as we readied to start our engines, our lieutenant called us over and said, "The president wants to thank you. Line up in single file."

President Truman walked up to each man in turn, who saluted and shook his hand. The president was in a cheerful mood and talked briefly to the officers. When he came up to me, I saluted smartly. As he took my hand, I remarked, "Thank you, sir, for the bomb. My division had been alerted to the Pacific."

President Truman hesitated for a moment. He looked straight into my eyes. I felt his hand squeeze tighter, and I knew he appreciated my comment.

Moments later, we were aboard our bikes. Motors roared, positions were taken, red lights flashed, and with sirens screaming we escorted the presidential party back to LaGuardia.

When I arrived home that evening, I told my family about the president's visit to New York—and that I spoke to him and shook his hand.

I can still see your Missouri smile, Mr. President. Rest in peace, Harry.

CHAPTER 7

The 87th Mountain Infantry Regiment: The Italian Campaign

On February 20, 1945, the 86th and 87th Mountain Infantry Regiments—supported by armor, artillery, and aircraft—launched an attack on Mount della Torraccio. Enemy resistance was fierce, but the position was finally taken after four days of bitter fighting.

On March 5, the 87th Mountain Infantry Regiment captured Castel d'Aiano. Meanwhile, the 85th seized Mount della Spe and cut the main German supply line to the Po Valley.

Melvin Borders Jr., Company A, 87th Mountain Infantry Regiment related his vivid story of the Italian campaign in King of the Mountain *(Minigraph #MG-706), published by Merriam Press. Borders's intriguing account has been edited with permission of the publisher.*

I joined the 10th Mountain Division at Camp Swift, Texas. I thought it was pretty flat country for mountain troops. I never did figure that one out. But the army, in its infinite wisdom, does strange things at times.

After basic training, I lied my way into the 10th. "Yes, I had skinned mules, and yes, I had skiing experience."

We arrived at Naples, Italy, in January 1945. The city was bustling with activity. All kinds of war materiel was piled high everywhere. Naples itself was literally a cesspool and off-limits to most military personnel. Young children could be seen pimping for their sisters for a candy bar or pack of cigarettes.

From Naples, we traveled by boat to Pisa and encamped for a period of time. From here, we were ordered out on a nighttime march to Vidiciatico. We trudged as quietly as hundreds of men could walk when loaded down with full packs. The word was passed—no smoking or lights of any kind.

It was still dark when we arrived at Vidiciatico. Some of us were billeted in private homes, but we were forbidden to go outside for fear of being seen by the enemy and jeopardizing any element of surprise for the forthcoming attack.

All the next day, we kept ourselves busy—sleeping, eating, cleaning rifles, dreaming of home, and preparing mentally for the battle ahead.

I peered out a window at the mountains that were to be our objective. It was February, and heavy, dark clouds hovering over the peaks only added to the tension.

At dark the next evening, our artillery began shelling the awesome mass looming in front of us—Mount Belvedere. The noise was deafening. We soon received word to move out in battle formation. We had advanced about four miles up the road when all hell broke loose. The Germans were answering our artillery with their own thunderous barrage.

I just kept moving forward, putting one foot in front of the other, even though my guts were churning. There was no moon, and the air was bitter cold. This was my first taste of combat, and I was scared to death.

The intensity of the shelling increased and was quickly joined by the incessant sound of German machine gun fire. I couldn't see anything except when flashes of gunfire lit up the scene. I knew there was an enemy soldier pulling the lanyards on the artillery pieces and squeezing the triggers on the machine guns, but I had yet to see any Germans.

Many thoughts raced through my mind. Would I be able to kill, and would I like it? That really scared me. What if I enjoyed killing?

We soon reached Querciola, a small village on the road to Corona. Enemy artillery shells kept whistling over our heads. They weren't close, but it was still a terrifying sound. You quickly learn to recognize the sound of shells with your name on them. You hit the deck and start praying.

We ducked into a house to escape the enemy artillery barrage and waited an hour hoping for the shelling to abate. Fat chance.

After a short time, we managed to force our way into Corona. The hamlet was situated on one side of Belvedere. During a house-to-house search, we lost one man when my squad entered a booby-trapped dwelling. Four dead German soldiers laid sprawled grotesquely in front of the stone building. I stood over them for a few moments to satisfy a curiousity as to my reaction. As I gazed at them, I was amazed at how detached I could be about death.

I had a chance to mull over the war while digging my foxhole in anticipation of more German shelling and a possible counterattack. Thinking is the soldier's enemy. We are taught to react automatically. If you have time to think about what you have done or are about to do, you're in real trouble.

In the infantry, the thinking is done for you. Your only duty is to obey orders. But now I was going through the hell of thinking about what I had done and what I had been through. I felt like a guy dumped in the ocean without a life preserver, watching my ship disappear over the horizon. What a lonely and helpless feeling.

We were soon ordered to move up to the crest of the mountain to take over previously dug defensive positions. We made the holes even deeper and strung wire—along with parts of C ration cans as an alarm system—all around our perimeter.

From this location, we were able to watch our planes bomb and strafe enemy positions in the valley below. Air support was not possible during our attack—or for several days after—because of bad weather.

We were jealous of the flyboys, mainly because they didn't have to fly under certain weather conditions. They could go back to their heated barracks and beds with clean sheets. We didn't consider them to be our equals—Just the guys who got all the glory, booze, and women. Lucky bastards!

Our artillery was constantly at work firing into the German lines. The shells made a friendly sound as they sailed over our heads. On one occasion, however, we were startled when they began falling on us. It seems that some of the guns had settled in the mud and were not accurately ranged. Luckily, nobody was killed or wounded.

We settled into a daily routine while waiting for a German counterattack in our sector, but it never came. We even had mail delivery, a few hot meals, a chance to write a letter or two, and a bath—GI-style. I probably should explain this procedure in the form of a recipe: First, pour one canteen of water into your steel helmet and brush your teeth. Then, shave using the same water. Next, take a sponge bath—without the sponge.

We carried water purification pills with us, so potable water wasn't a problem. However, all supplies had to be carried up to the front on the backs of mules or men. Water and ammunition were high priority. Food was secondary.

At night, when not on patrol or guard duty, I would wrap my blanket around me and curl up in my foxhole. I learned to breathe fast so that my warm breath served as a heater. Life under these conditions was pretty stark but bearable.

After two weeks on the front line, we were relieved of duty and trucked to Campo Tizzorro for a few days of rest and relaxation. I was able to take a hot shower and was sprayed for lice and issued new clothing.

We were quartered in a former nunnery for women. I had an army cot—no sheets, of course—but it was still luxury compared to living in a foxhole.

The one thing that impressed me most about this place was the john. It consisted of a hole drilled through a convex tile gutter with water running down the trough. On each side of the drain were impressions for your feet. To take a crap, it was necessary to squat directly over the hole.

But urinating was different. We had pissing contests to see who could hit the hole on the fly from the farthest distance. I never won.

Before going into combat, we would leave our duffel bags at a supply base. Each bag contained a mattress cover—the better-to-bury-you-in kind. Each soldier carried his own casket, so to speak.

Whenever we returned from the front lines, our duffel bags would be waiting for us. It was a pathetic and poignant scene, however, to watch as the last man retrieved his bag, because, sadly, it was not the last duffel bag. There were always many left—still sitting there—that belonged to the soldiers who had been killed or wounded. This was one way of learning who was no longer among us.

I remember one infuriating day at Campo Tizzorro when we were ordered to fall out with full battle gear for an overnight training exercise. Can you imagine that?! Battle-hardened veterans on a training exercise—and this while on R&R. What an insult. But that's the army for you.

Once a month if not in a combat area, we would be ordered to fall out in boots, raincoats, and helmet liners. That's all—not another stitch. Everyone knew what that meant—payday and "short-arm inspection." We would line up and face the medics. Each man was told to "skin it back and milk it down." The object of this examination was to prove that he didn't have the clap before claiming his pay. Woe be unto the soldier whose pecker leaked! This meant court-martial, forfeit of pay, and assorted other penalties. The army was tough on this, especially in combat areas. They didn't want guys shirking duty using a venereal disease as an excuse. In the army, it was difficult to be modest and survive.

During the month of March, we pressed the attack on the retreating Germans. They had formed a new defensive line farther north with the hinge at Castel d'Aiano. After a few attempts to take the town had been beaten back, my company was ordered to capture it with a frontal assault.

Boy, did we catch hell. The Germans were ready for us, firing 88s from protected positions in the hills. I hugged the earth for about six hours, trying to scratch a foxhole in the frozen ground with my helmet and bare hands. Through the morning mist, I could see the church tower with its big clock. The rest of the town was a pile of rubble.

We inched forward and finally managed to gain a foothold within the town itself. We fought our way through Castel d'Aiano and took up positions to the north.

We remained entrenched and under constant bombardment for about a week. At night the Germans would set up loudspeakers and broadcast their version of the latest news, telling of their victories and our defeats. Amazingly, they called us by regiment, company, and sometimes our names. They had one hell of a lot of information about us. I was intrigued by the chatter but was damn curious as to how they knew so much.

Nightfall was terror-time. We took turns at guard duty—two hours on, two or four off. The unlucky soldier was stationed at the point. This foxhole was situated about fifty to a hundred yards in front of our main line—sort of a forward warning system. You had to crawl on your belly to get there, and the rustle of every leaf became an enemy patrol.

Talking or even whispering to a foxhole buddy could be dangerous. And there was always the urge to take a piss. What a relief when the next shift showed up. Then you crawled back to the main line—never mind the fact that some poor bastard had to take your place. But, most of all, don't forget the password for the night or else you're one dead soldier.

Occasionally, when relieved from the front, we were sent to Pietra Colora. This wasn't exactly R&R since the town was still in the combat zone. But we could light up a cigarette without fear of being clobbered by enemy artillery. During the day, we sunbathed on the back side of the hill, even though the temperature was barely above freezing. We moved in and out of Pietra Colora several times and, in a way, the town became home to us.

On April 14, 1945, the big push began to chase the Germans out of Italy. We climbed into trucks and were driven to Mount Sinistero. Wow, was this place well named! We arrived about five o'clock in the morning and, at the first light of dawn, we could see the well-dug enemy positions facing us from across the valley.

This was the German's first line of defense. Our orders were to swarm over the ridge and take the mountain slopes in front of us. My company's assignment was to seize Torre Iussi, a small village on the left flank.

We knew that the enemy had every inch of the valley zeroed in with artillery, mortars, and machine guns. I remember talking to myself and wondering what my odds of survival were in this kind of situation.

Just before we attacked, trucks arrived packed with fresh troops. They were from the replacement depot and were to fill up our decimated ranks. These poor guys were about to get their first baptism under fire.

Our artillery barrage was lifted at dawn and replaced with .50-caliber machine guns that fired just over our heads. As we headed into this literal valley of death, I will never forget the sight—thousands of GIs pouring down the cliffs. The panorama reminded me of an old Civil War movie with lines of troops—bayonets fixed—advancing toward the enemy.

The roar of battle was overpowering. The ground shook as the Germans threw everything they had at us. We were helplessly pinned down for about five hours. The stench of death was everywhere. We inched forward on our bellies a little at a time—and prayed. We had to keep moving, though; otherwise enemy small arms and light machine gun fire would cut us to pieces.

Finally, about noon, we were able to get to our feet and advance up the road to Torre Iussi. Our dead were strewn everywhere At one place, a scattered group of body parts showed that apparently some of our guys made the mistake of clustering together and became targets of an enemy shell burst. The carnage was sickening. I tried to wipe the sights from my mind, but the pictures were too horrible.

By the time we reached Torre Iussi, most of the resistance in the village had been crushed. We took several German prisoners. They were a bitter group of men.

But there was little time to relax. We headed to the next ridge and dug in for the night. We always feared the dark because of enemy patrol activity, and there was also the chance of a counterattack. The Germans probably felt as we did, that the blanket of night was a great equalizer. We had the advantage during the day, but the odds were even during darkness.

There was not much time to rest or even think. Sleep was nearly impossible. When daylight came, we learned that two of our men had been knifed to death in their foxholes. It was kill or be killed. The Germans still had fangs of steel.

Throughout the morning and most of the afternoon, we hiked across another ridge. About five o'clock, we ran into fierce enemy resistance. A deadly wall of machine gun bullets and exploding mortar shells momentarily halted our advance.

My platoon was ordered to form a skirmish line and to lay down a base of fire above the heads of the other advancing platoons. Then it was our turn. We made it over the ridge, down the slope, across a gully, and up the next hill.

Enemy fire was murderous. Suddenly, directly in front of me, I saw two Germans lying in their foxhole with their rifles pointed at me. They could have blown my head off, but they were paralyzed with fear. My reaction was automatic. I had been well trained. I fired my rifle, wounding both of them.

As I looked up, I sighted a number of enemy soldiers coming down the hill with their arms high in the air—the traditional gesture of surrender. We didn't have time to handle them, so we motioned the Germans to the rear. Suddenly, I noticed this one fellow coming toward me—arms extended but still carrying his rifle. A grenade was attached to the weapon's barrel. I tensed up. He stopped, took aim, and pulled the trigger. I fired my gun at the same time. He dropped to the ground. I tried to take a step but couldn't move. I glanced down at my left leg. The thigh muscle had been blown away, and the bone was exposed. I collapsed to the earth. Surprisingly, my leg didn't hurt immediately. But then the pain rushed through me like a tidal wave. I couldn't move. I was in agony and bleeding all over the ground.

Weldon Storey found me. He tore off a piece of my clothing and twisted a tourniquet around my upper thigh. Minutes later a medic arrived and gave me a shot of morphine. What a relief! I felt like I was floating around and around in a warm whirlpool. I remember someone coming over to Weldon and telling him to stay with me. I was carefully put on a litter and carried down the hill. I was then hoisted onto the back of a jeep and strapped in.

The bumpy ride to the battalion aid station was tortuous. I winced at every turn of the wheel. At the aid station, I was placed on a table. A nurse asked me if I would like a shot of whiskey. I said, "Hell yes." I swallowed it in one gulp but puked it right back up.

I laid there in pain for what seemed hours. But after another shot of morphine, I didn't give a shit. I was loaded on another jeep for a trip to the 28th Evacuation Hospital.

I woke up in a bed with clean sheets. Slowly my wits returned to me. I remembered my leg. Did I still have it? I looked down the bed. They had saved it! What a beautiful sight—even with a cast all the way up to my crotch. I was deliriously happy and relieved. Then I fell into a deep sleep.

The next day, an army major showed up at the hospital. An enlisted man trailed behind him carrying a bunch of Purple Hearts. When they reached my bed, the officer presented me one of the medals and read the citation about how, since I was wounded in action, I was to be awarded the Order of the Purple Heart—carrying on the tradition from the days of George Washington.

The major seemed a bit nervous, and I was puzzled. Why all the rush to give me this medal? After all, I had been in the hospital only one day. The officer explained that it was the army's policy to make the presentations as quickly as possible to those men who had been seriously wounded in order to avoid posthumous awards. His remarks hit me like a brick. The son-of-a-bitch! True, my duffel bag would still be unclaimed if it wasn't for the fact I had survived a near-fatal injury. But, I made up my mind that the army wasn't going to put my body in a mattress cover no matter what this major thought. I didn't know it at the time, but I was on the critical list and not expected to make it.

Every time the doctors came around to examine my leg, they would place a towel over my face. A medic said they didn't want to upset me with the enormity of the wound. One day, I insisted on seeing the wound. I took one look then put the towel back across my eyes.

There were casualties from all branches of the service in our ward. One day, a medic wheeled in a member of the Army Air Corps. He was still wearing his jacket with three or four rows of citation bars pinned to his chest. Oak leaf clusters decorated many of the ribbons. I was impressed. Each oak leaf meant he had been awarded that particular citation more than once.

Wow! Here was a real hero. One of his legs was in a cast, and everyone crowded around wanting to know all the particulars about his injury. About this time, an officer hurried into the ward and gave him another decoration.

I don't know whether he was putting us on or not, but anyway this was his story. He had been brought to the hospital because his jeep had been involved in an accident and he had been thrown from the vehicle, breaking his leg.

Then the ax fell. I asked where he had seen all his action. He said that he had never been in any air battles. He was merely a cook for an air corps unit stationed far behind the lines. But every time his squadron even flew over a combat area, the entire unit received a citation. Boy, were we pissed! This only confirmed our opinion of flyboys and the favoritism they seemed to receive.

Closing my leg wound was accomplished in stages. I underwent four or five grafting operations. This took time, and boredom and tedium were the epitome of my hospitalization.

We looked forward to any little thing to enliven the day, and Fritz helped to fill the void in our humdrum life. I don't know if that was his real name or not. He was a German prisoner attached to my ward as a hospital orderly. Before the war, Fritz was a music teacher in Munich. Each morning we could hear him enter the building. He was always on time, and the precision clack-clack of his boots on the tile floor announced his arrival. He would march directly to the center of the ward, snap to attention, click his heels, and give us a stiff salute. A wide grin would spread across his face, like an actor anticipating a round of applause.

Fritz seemed glad to have been captured, but his main concern was for his hometown. He continually prodded information from anyone who might fill him in on the latest news. At quitting time, he would perform the same ritual in reverse. We looked forward to his routine, and it helped to brighten the monotonous days.

There were always a few Japanese-American soldiers in the ward. Their outfit saw a lot of combat, and the troops were well respected. One fellow in particular had been wounded in the groin and was told that he might lose his testicles. The poor guy was on the verge of tears. We tried to assure the soldier that he would be okay, but it was a tough job.

Then one morning, about 3 A.M., the entire ward was awakened by a sudden ear-splitting shout. Lights were snapped on, and nurses came running. Our Japanese friend was screaming and hollering with joy. He lay on the bed, covers thrown back, pointing with pride at his nice stiff erection. We all clapped and cheered. I don't know if the ability to "get it up" had anything to do with his recovery, but at least he didn't have to lose his balls.

The days dragged on. Movies, food, letters from home, and exploring one's navel became obsessions. The dull daily routine became just that, and there seemed to be no end to it.

Then one day I learned that I was to be evacuated to Naples for the trip home on a hospital ship. I was ecstatic. And on July 31, 1945, with a huge cast hugging me to the waist, I was carried aboard the *Algonquin*.

Today, I run marathons and am often asked how I can run distances with most of my left thigh muscle missing. My answer is that I just put one foot in front of the other—just as I did on Belvedere. Life is like that.

One of my ambitions during these past years was to return to Italy and relive my wartime experiences. And I finally traveled back there in March 1981.

I drove through Vidiciatico where we had assembled for our night attack on Mount Belvedere. I located the house where I stayed just prior to the assault.

From here I traveled up the road to Querciola and met an old man who told me that several American soldiers sought shelter in his house during the German bombardment on the night of the offensive. I remarked that I possibly may have been one of the Americans.

At Corona, I pinpointed almost the exact spot where I dug my foxhole. I recognized the site because it was picked as a good location to set up a machine gun.

From here, I could see the crest of Mount Belvedere, with its hump on one side and the ridge connecting it to another rugged mountain peak to the north.

My next stop was Castel d'Aiano. I was surprised to see that the church tower and clock had survived. I then located the field where I laid for hours while under heavy fire from German artillery. It's now a parking lot. Such is the progress of civilization.

I also visited the city square and saw the monument erected by the townspeople in honor of the American troops. The plaza is named the 10th Mountain Division Piazza Caduti (the plaza of those fallen in action).

Other towns on my itinerary were Pietra Colora, Campo Tizzorro, and Cutigliano. They were rest stops—or at least a sanctuary from the pressures of fighting for your life. They really hadn't changed that much—just more buildings and people.

I tried to find Torre Iussi but then learned that the place didn't exist anymore. The Carabinieri (Italian police) helped me locate the ruins. It was as I remembered—about five bombed-out buildings surrounding a small plaza. We captured a number of German soldiers here.

Today, Torre Iussi is only a ghostly memorial to the war. It stands in stark contrast to a small village that has grown up a short distance away. I crossed the road to view the valley where we had caught so much hell attacking the enemy's main line of defense. To my right was Mount Sinistero. To my left were the cliffs and the Germans. But now, the valley was peaceful and serene. A small church and several homes dotted the landscape.

As I surveyed the terrain, memories began flooding back from my subconscious. I remembered my friends who had been killed and wounded here. It was a bittersweet reunion. I was filled with ambivalent emotions—glad to see the battlefield again but terribly sad at the same time.

I found it hard to imagine how I lived through those days. And yet here I was, walking on the very ground that had been so bitterly contested.

Halfway down a newly paved road leading to the floor of the valley, a monument had been erected honoring the Americans who died in battle. Fresh flowers are placed there daily.

I talked with a farmer who lived nearby. He was fourteen years old at the time and said that he would never forgot the terrible carnage.

To the north, I could see the mountainous ridge where I was wounded. I was unable to get to the site, however, so had to be content with what I had already seen.

This was a trip I'll never forget. It was thrilling to see the mountains again. What happened here shaped my life and thinking. I am what I am today—the good and the bad—largely because of my experiences in Italy with the 10th Mountain Division.

George W. "Pete" Peterson was a rifle squad leader and platoon guide with Company I, 87th Mountain Infantry Regiment. His vivid accounts of the campaign in northern Italy have been edited with permission.

In mid-March 1945, Company I was occupying a defensive position in the general area of Montese. It was a quiet sector. This was a relief, since we had been pounded recently by enemy artillery for several days on the so-called Punch Board Hill. It had been correctly named—scarcely a yard of ground was without a shell hole.

After a short respite, however, Company I received orders to send out a platoon-sized patrol several miles behind enemy lines. The main purpose of the mission was to capture at least one German soldier.

Lieutenant Alexander Jones was assigned as patrol leader, and T/Sergeant Alexander Beauchesne was made assistant leader. Twenty-six other men were picked from the company. I was a sergeant in the first platoon when I was selected for the mission. We were armed to the teeth with MI rifles, BARS, pistols, and trench knives.

The plan seemed simple enough. We only had to cross a German minefield then head for some farmhouses where enemy activity had been observed. At the same time, an artillery barrage—including phosphorous shells—would be fired to force the Germans inside.

Sergeant Bill Eisendrath and his squad were picked to probe a safe lane through the mines. This took several nights, and the cleared path was marked with engineer tape.

At dark on March 19, our patrol carefully approached the enemy position. We crossed the minefield without incident. There was some moonlight, and the patrol advanced rapidly across the rolling farmland. I found hard to believe that we were actually moving unimpeded through German lines. It seemed more like a dream or training exercise.

We safely reached the predesignated position near our objective. It was three o'clock in the morning, and the enemy soldiers were evidently having breakfast. We could hear their voices and the dull clang of mess gear.

We spread out, took whatever cover we could find, and waited for the artillery barrage. Minutes later, shells began zooming over our heads and exploded with deafening roars in the target area.

As soon as the barrage was lifted, a squad and an interpreter, cautiously entered one of the farmhouses. After a careful search of the building, they found twenty-three Germans hiding in the cellar. They were a disheveled bunch of men—some even without boots. One soldier kept blubbering over and over again, "Don't shoot! Don't shoot!"

We lined the prisoners up in columns of three and headed back to our regiment. The Germans were forced to march in front in case we encountered any mines.

We returned safely without incident, and the patrol was cited as one of the most successful ever sent out in the Italian theater. Lieutenant Jones was awarded the Silver Star, and each NCO received the Bronze Star.

About the middle of April, the 10th Mountain began its push into the Po Valley. Company I was given the mission of seizing Mount Mosca and nearby Hills 779 and 787. My platoon was assigned to capture Hill 779. The hill rose nearly five hundred feet and extended about a thousand feet along its base.

As we spread out and advanced toward our objective, several men on the left of the line had to cross an open area. The rest of the platoon received some protection from a wooded area and a gully.

Suddenly, as we moved forward, an enemy sniper began firing at the unprotected men. John Spreng was shot. Barton Morrison, the platoon medic, hurried to his aid but was also struck down. The sniper kept shooting at the two fallen soldiers, even though the red cross on the medic's helmet was clearly visible.

Willard Nichols and I—using the gully as cover—were able to sneak within several yards of Spreng and Morrison, but they appeared dead and didn't respond when we called out to them. I realized that it would be foolhardy to try to attempt a rescue—especially since the sniper continued to use them for target practice. When the bodies of the two men were recovered, both had multiple gunshot wounds. Morrison had been shot more than twenty times.

As we continued our advance, no enemy fire was received from the forward slope of Hill 779. With the First Squad in the lead, my platoon moved cautiously along a narrow dirt road at the base of the hill.

Suddenly, a German officer rounded a bend in the path. He had a machine pistol slung over his neck and was carrying a map case. I was caught by surprise and automatically opened fire. After the smoke had cleared—so to speak—I was amazed to see the German still standing with his weapon hanging in two pieces. The surprised officer exclaimed in perfect English, "Boy, you almost got me!"

Soon after this startling episode, enemy artillery zeroed in on the forward slope. Our platoon rapidly spread out on the back side of the hill. Shrapnel from exploding shells wounded three of our men—Denzel Carrico, Harry Arcado, and Vito Acciarito.

Meanwhile, the sniper continued his work. Ed Vitalius was struck in the leg, and a bullet ploughed up the ground a few inches from my position.

Then, just before dusk, I saw Orville Cockrill—armed with a BAR—herding the captured sniper to the rear. I remarked to Cockrill that this was the person who killed Morrison and Spreng. Minutes later, a shot rang out near our command post. When asked what happened, Orville replied that his prisoner had tried to escape. The sniper's body was found in a ditch alongside the road.

On April 21, the Third Battalion of the 87th Mountain Infantry Regiment was moving north through the Po Valley when it encountered heavy enemy fire. The battalion commander ordered Company I to clear a German force from a row of stone farmhouses in the village of Manzolino.

As additional firepower, two Sherman medium tanks were attached to our company. And a couple of light machine guns from Company M were mounted on the hoods of two jeeps and secured with sandbags.

One platoon of Company I was ordered to clear the farmhouses on the left. Then suddenly, as the rest of the company moved forward, the distinctive sound of German tank tracks could be heard. Minutes later, an enemy tank was sighted moving slowly through a grassy field dotted with fruit trees. The tank stopped opposite the farmhouses and opened fire with machine guns.

A ten-foot-high irrigation dike ran in a north-south direction in front of the dwellings for a distance of about a hundred yards, then curved east. One unit of Company I was positioned on top of the dike, while another section was stationed in front of the embankment facing the German.

Our two Shermans were sitting out in the open at the lower end of the dike. The jeeps armed with machine guns pulled up on the dike and poured out a steady stream of bullets at the enemy. The jeep gunners seemed oblivious to the danger of their exposed position and wore ski caps instead of steel helmets. The noise must have sounded like rain on a tin roof to the Germans inside the tank.

But the enemy was so busy shooting at the farmhouses that they didn't notice the Sherman tanks about a hundred yards to the south. We assumed that our tank gunners would quickly knock out the Germans, but they didn't open fire.

Captain Riordan was furious. He shouted at the Sherman crews to shoot. One of the tanks finally got a shot off, but it missed the target by fifty yards. Now, however, they were noticed. The German tank's turret slowly rotated in our direction. It fired one 88mm round, slicing off the gun barrel of one of the Shermans. This was the signal for our tank crews to "abandon ship."

Meanwhile, the Company I riflemen, and the Company M machine gunners, kept spraying the Germans with bullets. Moments later, the enemy tank got off another round. The shell crashed through the dike's ten-foot wall of dirt and exited the other side.

However, the Germans failed to notice our men dug in along the front of the dike. The tankers were probably too busy firing at the farmhouses to notice our troops practically under their guns.

The standoff was broken when Willard Nichols crawled unnoticed up to the enemy tank and disabled it with an antitank grenade. Evidently that was enough. The Germans climbed out of the tank waving a white flag. Nichols was awarded the Silver Star for his act.

With the tank obstacle now out of the way, our battalion deployed along both sides of the north-south road and advanced toward the town of Bastiglia. Just before dark, an enemy plane roared in low over our column. One of our machine gunners fired a short burst at the aircraft. The German aircraft then circled wide and made another run at us.

Someone shouted, "Get off the road!" Most of the men took cover on either side of the pathway. But a number of soldiers took refuge in a nearby two-story stone house. The pilot dropped a few bombs. One scored a direct hit on the dwelling, killing fourteen men and wounding thirty. Thus ended another relaxing day on our tour of the beautiful Italian countryside.

On April 23, we assembled in the vicinity of the San Benedetto Bridge and prepared to cross the Po River. The sharp crack of antiaircraft fire could be heard, and deadly puffs of smoke from airbursts could be seen.

Some units of the 87th Mountain Infantry Regiment had already crossed the river on pontoon boats. During the crossing, they were under continuous attack from German artillery. Fortunately, by the time Company I climbed into the boats, there was a lull in enemy fire, and we reached the far bank without incident.

After crossing the Po, we headed a few miles inland to a small town and established a defense perimeter for the night.

The next morning, Company I was given the job of locating and destroying the pesky enemy guns. As we moved west—parallel to the river—our platoon came under attack from small arms. My squad quickly established a base of fire, while other units flanked the enemy. Two German soldiers were captured.

We soon reached the top of an irrigation ditch. The rest of the company spread out along a small wooded stream about thirty yards to the rear. Minutes later, my squad began receiving enemy fire from the right flank.

While we were busy countering the enemy attack, three Germans stood up on the dike and started shooting at our troops positioned along the stream. The Germans had blackened faces, were dressed in camouflage uniforms, and were wearing ski caps. However, they were so intent on firing at our men by the river that they didn't notice my squad deployed several yards away.

The Germans suddenly pulled back from the dike. As they withdrew, I shot the last man as he tried to escape. During the firefight, John W. Haines III was killed when he moved forward to reposition his machine gun. Edward Myers, Bruno Guido, and Daniel Walsh were wounded.

It soon became evident that the enemy attack was a ruse to cover the withdrawal of their artillery. By the time our company regrouped, the Germans had successfully left the area.

In retrospect, it was obvious that the virtually unopposed crossing of the Po River was the direct result of General Hays's strategy of driving his forces ahead so fast that it was impossible for the enemy to establish a solid line of defense. In fact, the Germans were unable to hold an extensive system of concrete trenches they had constructed on the north shore of the Po in the vicinity of the San Benedetto crossing.

General Hays disregarded warnings that both his flanks were exposed. But evidently, he thought along the same lines as General George Patton—who, when told that his flanks were exposed, snarled the famous remark, "Fuck flank security! Let the enemy worry about his own flanks!"

One of the many stories making the rounds after the German surrender concerned a forty-year-old private by the name of Johnny Grantham. Johnny was a tall, cold-eyed Texan and a member of the First Platoon of Company I. (I later learned that he had been a professional gambler in civilian life.)

We always had blackjack games going on at every opportunity, especially after payday. Johnny constantly tried to get into the games but was usually barred because he never lost.

Anyway, or so the story goes, Johnny was drinking at a bar with a few friends when a huge, mean, drunken soldier lurched through the door. The stranger staggered up to the first man he saw and demanded angrily, "What outfit are you from?!" The intimidated soldier calmly replied, "The 91st Pinetree Division." With that, the drunk hauled off and slugged the fellow.

The bar quickly became quiet as the interloper pushed his way up to another soldier and exclaimed, "What's your division?!" The young fellow's voice faltered as he answered, "The 34th Division." And he was immediately knocked to the floor.

While all this was going on, Johnny had pulled out a foot-long switchblade knife and nonchalantly began paring his fingernails. The drunk quickly noticed the silent Texan and belligerently growled at him, "What's your division?!"

As Johnny turned slowly toward the inebriated soldier, the sharp point of his knife blade rested inches from the big guy's belly. Johnny looked the man straight in the eye and said, "I reckon, I'm from the 10th Mountain Division!" The drunk sobered up in a hurry when he looked down at the knife and answered, "Now that's a good division. Let me buy you a drink!"

In his memoirs, John Fitzgerald recounted an interesting story about the 10th Mountain "Mule Corps" in Italy.

We had many mules and mule skinners in the 87th. When I arrived at Fort Lewis, Washington, the entrance to the regimental area had a large sign overhead that read "87th Mountain Infantry Regiment Reinforced." A few inches below was printed "Through These Portals Pass the Most Beautiful Mules in the World."

The animals were used at Camp Hale to haul supplies, although the artillery utilized most of them for carrying ammunition. However, the mules didn't do well in deep snow. The had to keep to the roads and paths. The Studebaker Weasel was better—but not much.

We took six thousand mules to Italy, but they were never used. Instead, we used mules belonging to the Italian partisans. There was a good reason for this. The partisans would remove the vocal chords from their mules, making them mute. Naturally, we couldn't do that to our animals. The ASPCA would have had a fit.

But the Italian mules did a great job. Not one bray or whinny to give our positions away. However, some good probably came of this. I imagine that many an impoverished Italian farm was enriched by a noisy U.S. Army mule.

John Fitzgerald continued his memoirs by recalling his experiences with the 87th Mountain Infantry Regiment in Italy.

When we first went into the field, we were bivouacked on the grounds of King Victor Emmanuel's hunting lodge but still near enough to the front to hear artillery fire in the distance.

One of my first duties was to escort seven prisoners to division headquarters. They were just young scared kids and walked in front of me, hands on heads. As we headed toward the rear, the attitude of our troops toward the prisoners became militant. The farther from the front, the more belligerent were their remarks, such as, "What are you bringing them back for? You should have killed the bastards!"

There was one guy who wasn't even a soldier and got me real mad. He was a cameraman from Fox Movie-Tone News. He stopped me and asked if I could march the prisoners down a different path. He wanted to film them walking between the ruins of a building and an overturned German tank.

After he took his picture, the cameraman went up to one of the prisoners and yanked the man's watch off his wrist. I hit the ceiling, but there was nothing I could do but cuss him out. The photographer was wearing a war correspondent's uniform—similar to an officer's—but no insignia. It was a pitiful display of arrogance.

On another occasion, I was asked to squire around the well-known photographer Margaret Bourke-White. I escorted her to Punch Board Hill, where she took pictures of two dead Germans. I also enlisted Torger Tokle and a few other skiers to perform for photos. Torger couldn't find the proper bindings for his skis and used an old necktie.

What I noticed the most about Bourke-White was the ashen look on her face, evidently caused by her flight. She had flown to Italy on an army air force transport, and part of her gear included several cases of flashbulbs. Somewhere over the ocean, the bulbs began exploding, probably from static electricity. Emergency foam immediately filled the cabin, and everyone aboard the aircraft was visibly shaken.

I remember the night when we were ordered out on a forced march. No smoking, no talking, no nothing except walking in double file along a narrow mountain road. A patch of flourescent tape was attached to each soldier's rucksack to guide the man behind him. I dozed off a few times and bumped into the soldier ahead of me. I learned from this experience that it was possible—on a forced march—to fall asleep while putting one foot in front of the other.

We soon arrived at a large school building and were directed to the gymnasium to wait for further orders. At dawn, we were told that we were free to sleep, eat, smoke, and use the indoor toilets, but we were prohibited from going outside, even for a second.

Throughout the day and the next night, there was nothing to do except write letters or get in one of the card games that always spring up at every opportunity.

The following morning, we marched back to the same place we had left. Months later, I heard that we were the reserve unit for the attack on Riva Ridge. Long after the war, a famous racehorse was named Riva Ridge after the famous battle.

We were often billeted in buildings or homes in the various small mountain towns. One place I'll never forget was Catigliano—a postcard-type village on the top of a mountain. It could only be reached by a steep winding road.

My squad was quartered in a hotel, the Pension Suisse. A small section of its roof was missing, but otherwise the building was in good shape. The cooks set up field ranges in the kitchen, and we ate in style in the dining room.

An old church was situated near the village square. Its facade was inlaid with ceramic tiles that depicted family crests and coats of arms of the English who passed through here on one of the Crusades.

Across the valley was a sister village occupied by the Germans. One power station served both communities with electricity, and neither side wanted to knock out the station. After all, there was no point in both towns suffering.

My first night on guard duty at Catigliano, I was ordered to set up a light machine gun on a tripod. This was kind of ridiculous, because I didn't even know how to operate the damn thing.

Our line of defense consisted of trip wires and flares. We didn't have long to wait before the alarm went off. Parachute flares shot in the sky. The dark Mountainside became bright as day, but nothing was moving. The only sound was a few tiles falling off a roof, and then all was quiet.

The next morning an investigation was held into the incident, but no official answer was given. However, we soon learned what really happened.

The Germans had occupied Catigliano for a long time and knew the town like a book. A person could go anywhere in the village by way of the roofs. The enemy soldiers were well acquainted with the buildings—including the local brothel. It seems they got the hots that night and sneaked back to get laid. Some war!

About this time, the enemy began conserving ammunition. They would send a round or two our way now and then just to keep us on our toes. One afternoon, a random German artillery shell shot up our church bell tower. That really got us mad. Our gunners spent thousands of bucks popping away until they finally knocked off the other town's bell tower. Revenge is sweet!

On another occasion, four of us were billeted in a small house that belonged to a mom and pop and their five-year-old daughter, Rosa. Pop had served in the Italian Air Force and had been shot down in the Ethiopian campaign.

One night while sitting around the living room—with a hot fire blazing and sipping the house vino—I took out my writing pad and began sketching. Pop liked my drawings and asked if I would do a portrait of his daughter. I did a pen-and-ink sketch that accidently turned out very good. I signed the drawing and received kisses and hugs from the whole family.

Pop was very grateful. He jabbered something in Italian, then rushed downstairs to the cellar. We could hear him scrounging around for a few minutes, then he returned with two large, dust-covered bottles. He carefully poured each of us a glass of the most delicious wine I have ever tasted. Pop said that he didn't know how old it was, but I sensed he had saved it for special occasions. The wine was pink in color, and, to use a wine taster's expression, "It has body!"

We spent another couple of nights in a village near the town of Pistola. I thought it strange that the citizens didn't know the pistol was born there.

Anyway, this village was built vertically up the face of a mountain. Many of the streets were actually stairways. The platoon sergeant and I shared a bedroom on the top floor of a house. The local church was on the street below us, but its bell tower was level with our window.

On our first night in the village, an old woman died about two o'clock in the morning. The church bells immediately went crazy. Bong! Bong! Bong! You could hear them ring in Brooklyn. The noise was deafening. Our brains were scrambled. My hearing has never been the same since.

Sleep was impossible, so we got up and joined the local throng. Everyone was milling about—except the coffin maker, who took his measurements and then hurried back to his shop.

My squad was ordered to go to the dead woman's home. The corpse was laid out on a bed in the living room. A candle was burning on each bedpost. A priest soon arrived and led the recitation of the rosary.

It was about noon when the coffin maker finished his job and the body was carried to the church. A high mass was performed by a visiting priest.

These centuries-old towns were originally built as forts, and the cemetery was about two miles away, so naturally everyone walked to the graveyard. Coming from a family of undertakers, I had more than a passing interest in the local ritual. The procession was interesting, to say the least.

First came the altar boys, swinging incense bottles and sprinkling holy water. They were followed by the priests—dressed in red and gold vestments—then the pallbearers carrying the coffin on their shoulders. Bringing up the rear were the men of the village. They were bareheaded and were followed by the women, wearing hats and veils.

After the graveside service, everyone was invited to the town square. The vino was brought out, and we all mourned the passing of a prominent person of the village.

One interesting detail about this house we were quartered in was the toilet. It was on the bottom floor and just off the wine cellar. The toilet was situated in a small closet with no door. It consisted of a marble bench with a ten-inch hole that was covered with a heavy, ornate marble stopper.

It didn't take long to figure out how the plumbing worked. The houses were all multilevel, and we noticed an iron door at the sidewalk level of our building. None of us had the guts to open it.

One local lady we got to know was a young camp follower. She cycled around town on a rickety bicycle and was called "Buono Snatch." Her parents were affectionally known as "Poppa and Momma Snatch."

I remember the time when there was a lull in the fighting, and we moved up to the front to replace a Brazilian unit. We always exercised complete blackouts if there was any possibility of being observed by the enemy. However, these boys from Brazil all smoked cigars out in the open, and the officers used flashlights to show us our positions. We could hardly wait for them to leave, and they were glad to go.

Several days later, I learned what was really happening and how they were able to get away with such dangerous activity. It seems that the German soldiers—whose families were bombed out of their homes—could request leave time from the front. Their timing was superb. They were allowed to go as a unit and be replaced by another outfit returning from leave. A transfer of this kind was taking place the night we relieved the Brazilians.

We occupied two-man foxholes and took turns sleeping and staying awake. Malfred Heimer didn't have a buddy in his dugout and fell asleep. He awoke about dawn and noticed three men standing nearby. They were talking in low voices. Malfred wrapped a blanket around his shoulders and, without taking his rifle or helmet, walked over to them.

"Hi, fellas," he said. "Anyone got a cigarette?" Malfred got the shock of his life when he heard "Achtung!" followed by a jumble of other German words. He was immediately taken prisoner and marched to the enemy lines.

Bob Dudley saw the whole thing. He woke Charles Ernst—Malfred's squad leader—and reported what happened. Charlie was really upset. He had just been promoted to squad leader. His new job was now in jeopardy. Charlie exclaimed, "Damn it! We better get him back! The captain will be pissed!"

Bob and Charlie carefully followed the Germans and their prisoner. Malfred was taken inside a pink stucco house. However, Ernst and Dudley were now in a quandry—what to do next? They had come too far to rush back to company headquarters and get help. And, even if they did, any rescue attempt might endanger Heimer's life.

What to do? There were at least three enemy soldiers in the building. You can't just go up and knock on the door—can you? But that's exactly what they did. Bob pounded on the door as hard as he could and shouted, "Malfred, are you in there?"

Loud, angry mumbling was heard inside the house, and a German opened the door. Bob and Charlie pointed their rifles at him. The fellow was taken by surprise, and an entire enemy squad came out with their hands raised. Malfred was still wrapped in his blanket and kept calling out, "Don't shoot! Don't shoot! It's me!"

These Germans had become lost while trying to locate their replacements when they stumbled upon Malfred. Charlie told me later that the enemy soldiers were not too happy when they realized that they had been bluffed by only two Americans.

My artistic talents were often called upon in many strange ways. After being in bivouac for any length of time, we had to cover our open latrines with dirt. And since I was the company Leonardo Da Vinci, I was called upon to produce a piece of artwork—usually on a scrap of wood—that carried the following message: "Latrine Closed, [the date], Company I, 87th Mountain Infantry Regiment." I don't know how many of these signs I created, but I understand that none of them are hanging in museums.

There was one latrine that was dug alongside a little-used road. It seems that Bob Diehl and I picked the same time to use the facility. With toilet tissue tucked into our helmets, we squatted back to back as we straddled the trench. Suddenly, Bob shouted, "Via! Via!" I quickly turned around and saw two nuns—dressed in their black habits—asking for chocolate and cigarettes.

The morning of March 3, 1945, dawned bright and clear. I'll never forget the day. We were dug in just down the mountain from Pietra Colora. Our attack began at 7 A.M. with a flight of dive-bombers blasting enemy positions. It was followed by a twenty-minute artillery barrage.

We shoved off a few minutes later along with other companies of the 87th and units of the 86th. Our third platoon led the advance in our sector. We moved up a narrow road that rose sharply to the right and, on our left, dropped off to a grove of olive trees.

We made good progress for several minutes until we heard the unmistakable chatter of a burp gun. This held us up for awhile, but we managed to get rid of the nuisance in short order.

As we continued to advance, the Germans decided that this would be a good time to rake us with artillery fire. Enemy salvos exploded on all sides. We huddled together against the crest of the hill and kept a low profile. The explosions were continuous and deafening. The shelling only lasted a few minutes, but it seemed like hours. All of us were covered with dirt. Nobody stirred. At first, I thought everyone else was dead. Suddenly, my right leg began to hurt like hell. Then I heard Bob Diehl call out, "Anybody need a medic?" That's when I realized I had been hit.

Minutes later, the medics arrived. I was placed on a litter, given a shot of morphine, and carried down the slope until we were safe from enemy fire. I was handed some sulfa tablets to take with a full canteen of water. But there was one small problem. My canteen was filled to the brim with vino. An understanding medic came to my aid with a full canteen of water.

I managed to sit up to look at my leg. There was a large blood stain with bright, white shards sticking through my ski pants. They were bone splinters from my tibia.

We suddenly began receiving small arms fire. I could feel flying dirt and stones strike the back of my parka. We got out of there fast. My litter bearers soon reached about the same place where I had started from earlier in the morning. I noticed our weapons platoon was lined up waiting to move forward.

I was the first wounded man of the day to be evacuated, and the word quickly spread—not just who I was, but the extent of my injury. It seems I had received what was called a "million-dollar wound"—not life-threatening, but bad enough to keep me out of action for a long time.

I was carried to the battalion aid station where my leg was wrapped in a chicken-wire splint. I complained of dry mouth but was told it was caused by the shot of morphine I received.

Then, to prepare me for the jeep ride to the battalion collecting station, a medic placed a fat gauze sponge—laced with bourbon—on my tongue.

It was a short, uneventful ride except for one incident. As we approached a main road, the jeep driver pulled over to the side and stopped. He looked at his watch, lit a cigarette, and offered one to me. When I asked about the delay, he answered, "Wait four minutes and you'll see."

The driver explained that German artillery had this crossroad zeroed in. And, every twenty minutes after the hour, they would shell the hell out of it. Sure enough, right on time, a few salvos landed right on the road.

As soon as the smoke cleared, we were on our way again. The jeep driver carefully passed over the shell holes, and we hurried on to the collecting station.

I didn't get more bourbon here, just a better splint. Also, a small wooden sign was wired to my parka. It had a large red "S" for surgery printed on it.

I was then put aboard an ambulance for transfer to a field hospital. It had been moved up from Anzio the day before. A German medic prisoner was with me. By this time, the morphine was beginning to wear off, and I was in pain. Every time the ambulance hit a bump, the medic would show me his Geneva Conference Noncombatant Red Cross card. That didn't help much. What I really needed was another shot of morphine.

I think I was one of the first patients brought into the hospital. I was quickly placed on an examining table. A nurse and surgeon came over to me. The doctor asked if I hurt any other place than my leg. I answered that my left elbow was stiff and sore. Then I raised the arm, and blood poured out from the sleeve of my parka.

My clothes were immediately cut off. I was x-rayed and carried to the operating room. A surgical team came in, introduced themselves, and began asking questions. Minutes later, I heard someone running across the duckboard floors. It was a medic with my x-rays. I anxiously watched the surgeons as they studied the still dripping films.

My next cognitive memory was of waking up at dark and in terrible pain. Then came more shots, and I kept weaving in and out of consciousness. When my fog-covered mind began to clear, I saw two familiar faces looming over me—Charlie Ernst and Anthony Kowalczyk.

Charlie had been hit in the ass by a large piece of shrapnel. Another shell fragment had punctured the front of Tony's helmet but stopped at his forehead. He was in the hospital for a couple of days with a bad headache. They sat by my bedside for a few hours waiting for me to wake up. Good friends.

I noticed my right leg was in a plaster cast from my crotch to my toes. And my left arm was in a cast from my shoulder to my fingers. I was given whole blood, plasma, saline, and glucose intravenously. After a couple of days, I was moved to another hospital. It formerly had been a TB sanitarium for children and overlooked the beach at Leghorn.

I went through several surgical procedures here—changing drains and that sort of stuff. In fact, I began to look forward to the sodium pentathol injections. One shot in the morning and you're out of it, then wake up ready for lunch. I also got a shot of penicillin every three hours around the clock.

The doctors told me that the shrapnel in my leg was from a large bore artillery shell, and my elbow wound came from a jacketed bullet. I also learned that Torger Tokle—the champion ski-jumper—was killed on the same day I was hit.

I'll always remember the day a nursing supervisor informed me that I was going home, and I was carried aboard a hospital ship for an eighteen-day voyage to Charleston, South Carolina.

While aboard ship, I heard the amazing story of Maurice "Speed" Murphy. Speed was a squad leader with the 85th Regiment. And, instead of a left arm, he only had a stump below the elbow. A soldier from Murphy's company told me how Speed lost his arm.

It seems that Speed's company had been relieved from the front and trucked to a building behind the lines for a shower, clean clothing, and a hot meal.

But, as Speed and his squad were taking off their packs, one soldier dropped a live grenade. Everyone dashed for cover as the grenade sizzled on its four-second timer. Speed was the nearest man to the explosive. He grabbed the grenade in his left hand and was about to hurl it out an open window when he saw a nun leading a group of toddlers past the building.

Speed's reaction was immediate. He pushed his left arm out the window and held it tight against the wall. The explosion shook the building and slammed his body to the ground—minus his left arm.

According to one story, as the medics were carrying Speed to the hospital, he joked, "Oh well, I can always get a job as a night watchman!"

Speed Murphy was a natural-born comic. He always addressed the nurses as "Loo-tenat," then held up the stump of his arm and removed the bonnet-type bandage—like tipping his hat.

CHAPTER 8

The 110th Mountain Signal Company: The Italian Campaign

On April 14, 1945, the 10th Mountain Division launched its spring offensive against enemy positions in the hills north of Mount della Spe. The Germans were prepared for the attack, and the 10th Mountain suffered its bloodiest day of the campaign. Among the casualties was Lieutenant Bob Dole, Company I, 85th Regiment, who was seriously wounded on Hill 913.

During the heavy fighting, Private John Magrath, Company G, 85th Regiment, knocked out four German machine guns on Hill 909. He then volunteered for another mission in which he was killed by enemy mortar fire. For his heroism, Magrath received the Medal of Honor—the only one awarded to a member of the 10th Mountain Division.

Daniel Dean Becker served with the 110th Signal Company and recalled the high and low points of life as a signalman.

I had six weeks of basic signal corps training at Camp Crowder. It wasn't too strenuous—mainly pole climbing, field telephone repair, and teletype maintenance.

After completing the course, I was sent with a group of other signalmen to Chicago to learn "automatic dial central office repair."

We were billeted at the local YWCA—with floor restrictions, of course—and marched every morning to the Automatic Electric Company for classwork instruction. There were several breaks for refreshments during the day, and we were served lemonade and cookies by pretty hostesses. This was heaven while it lasted.

From Chicago, we were sent to Camp Carson, Colorado, to await our next assignment. To alleviate the boredom—and keep us out of trouble—we were kept busy marching in close-order drill about eight hours every day.

It wasn't long before I received orders to report to Maryville, California, for a South Pacific assignment. But there was one problem. No Pacific outfit needed an automatic telephone switchboard repairman.

So, while the army brass hats were trying to figure out what to do with me, I was put to work—along with a few other men—walking the artillery range and marking unexploded shells with flags.

One day, while stopping for a break under a shade tree, I heard a chipping sound. I looked up just in time to see a soldier busy knocking the encrusted dirt off a live .37mm shell. I guess he wanted a souvenier. Well, it only took about a millisecond for five of us to jump on him, grab his arms, and teach him a lesson.

I immediately realized that this wasn't the safest job in the world. And, when the local government asked the army for volunteers to help with the peach crop, I quickly forgot my golden rule: "Never volunteer for nothing!"

There were only ten of us who signed up for the four days of hazardous duty. We slept on the floor of a high school gym and worked twelve hours a day pouring sugar syrup into cans of peaches.

We were only paid the minimum wage, but there were benefits—like meeting the local girls who worked at the cannery. It didn't take long for the word to get out about this good deal, and the next batch of volunteers numbered about ten thousand. For some reason, I wasn't picked anymore and had to go back to my artillery shells.

The army kept trying to find a place for me, and I was finally ordered to Norfolk, Virginia, to see if anyone in the European theater needed an automatic telephone switchboard repairman.

Well, it so happened that the 110th Mountain Signal Company, 10th Mountain Division, was shipping out and was one man short. They may not have wanted me, but they had no choice.

Once we were on the high seas, the captain called me to his quarters and—in no uncertain terms—expressed his disbelief that I had been assigned to the outfit.

First of all, he said that my training had nothing to do with the company's operation. After all, I hadn't marched twenty miles a day—with full pack, in below-zero temperatures, or slept on frozen tundra.

My only experience, in this regard, was a five-mile hike on a summer day with no pack. And my only overnight ordeal was as a Boy Scout.

The captain, however, was unimpressed and asked me what I did before joining the army. I told him that I worked on a farm and raised cattle.

The officer smiled from ear to ear and said, "Great, I have just the job for you—company mule skinner." In other words, I would be taking care of the company's animals.

The North Atlantic winter cruise to Italy took fourteen days. There was only one problem. Our sleeping quarters were directly under the movie theater. The same film ran continuously—twenty-four hours a day—and featured Lucille Ball and the song "Buckle Down Winsockie." In fact, I could remember the entire dialogue of the movie for the next ten years.

After docking at Naples, we went aboard an LCI (Landing Craft Infantry) for a trip north up the coast. A cold winter gale was blowing. My bed was the top bunk in the forward part of the ship, and at the exact spot where the fuel exhaust pipe entered the compartment. For some reason, the pipe was one foot short from being vented through the overhead deck plates.

The exhaust pipe was sucking air in and out at about sixty decibels. That, plus the fumes from diesel oil, would soon make everybody sick unless a solution was found—and fast. Signalmen are naturally quick to react. We collected about twenty pounds of dirty shorts and socks and jammed them into the vent pipe. We were now able to sleep reasonably well. Amazingly, the engine didn't stall out.

Upon arriving at Pisa, we were transported to "Pup-Tent City." I was surprised that the tents of an entire division would be set up so close to the front. I thought that dispersion would have been the rule.

I was issued a down-filled sleeping bag and would have received shoepac boots, but they didn't have my size. Instead I was given a pair of thin, five-buckle boots.

Just before we moved up to the front, General Hays ordered all sleeping bags taken away from us. Apparently, they would take too long to unzip in case of an emergency. I was also told that mountain men fight better when they're cold.

Well, I made up my mind that I wasn't going to freeze to death and fabricated my own sleeping bag. I laced up two blankets inside a mattress cover, leaving an opening at one end to crawl into. Fortunately, the general never saw my innovation, and I doubt if he would have appreciated my creativity.

The signal corps troops were issued the light, semiautomatic .30-caliber carbines. We trained with these weapons and had them zeroed in for accuracy. But, a couple of days before moving up to the front, we received a new model. There wasn't any procedure to zero in the adjustable sights, and we had to trust our lives to the factory calibration.

My wire chief, Lauren Bostwick, solved the problem. He scrounged up several jeeps so we could drive to a nearby hill and zero in the carbines on tin cans. I can still hit the side of a barn on occasion.

The regiment's artillery battery switchboard (about forty lines) was mounted in a 6x6 truck. It handled the telephone communications to the forward outposts, regimental command centers, and division and corps headquarters.

My job at the time was still mule skinner, when I heard through the grapevine that communications—at the regimental level—were breaking down.

The wire chief and other experts were unable to locate the problem. There was serious cross talk between circuits, and the hand crank often caused the wrong circuit to respond. The situation quickly became desperate. Then someone remembered the new man they picked up in Norfolk who had advanced switchboard training. But where was he? Well, he was busy feeding and taking care of the mules.

A frantic officer with a jeep was sent to pick me up, and I was briefed on the problem on the way to the front. At first, I figured that dust might be the cause. But, after opening the switchboard and blowing air into it, the trouble still existed.

Now was the time for prayer and enlightenment. My thoughts were suddenly directed away from the switchboard to a string of lightning protectors for the incoming lines. Each protector consisted of two half-inch carbon plates with a mica gasket that provided a 5/1000 of an inch space between the carbon plates. One plate was connected to the ground, while the other was fastened to one of the lines. Any high-voltage spike would jump across the mica gap and be directed to the ground, thereby protecting the switchboard and the telephone operator. Repeated lightning arcs would cause a carbon buildup across the gap, resulting in cross talk between circuits.

I thought this might be the problem, and within a few minutes I had pulled out the carbon blocks, cleaned the mica gap, and reinstalled the blocks. The problem was solved, and I was rewarded. I never had to see another mule.

One evening during the spring offensive, I went with some friends to explore a nearby hill and search for souvenirs. We soon came upon a half-dozen enemy dead in front of a farmhouse. We climbed down the basement stairs and into a room loaded with all kinds of stuff. I collected a few German and Italian field telephones, along with repair manuals. To this day, I don't know why.

I was the last man to leave the basement. As I climbed the stairs, I got the shock of my life. Staring at me under the fifth step from the top was a German hand grenade with a trip wire. The wire had been set too far back on the step, and the heels of our boots missed it by less than an inch.

Another one of my unusual experiences was a telephone conversation I had with a high-ranking officer. My job during the spring campaign was to man the switchboard. I never received training for this, but I could say "operator" and plug in the correct extension. For some reason, I was assigned the 3 A.M. to 6 A.M. shift—probably because I was the new kid on the block.

As I remember the incident, it had been an exhausting day during the German retreat. I was trying to stay awake—at four o'clock in the morning—while answering a ten-line battery switchboard. At the time, my location was at the farthest point of the telephone line from corps headquarters. The phone rang, I answered "operator," and the conversation went something like this:

"Connect me to General Hays."

"Can't do. They went north. No telephone communication as yet."

"What's your location, son?" I gave him my position.

"Are you sure, son," he answered. "It can't be!"

"Yes sir. General Hays passed by here about six hours ago."

"Great work, son! When you see your general tell him I called."

Then I pulled the plug. I never did get the name of the person I was talking to.

There was one outfit that provided hot showers for the troops. On occasion, we would take advantage of the facility to wash off the dirt and grime and get clean clothing.

It was a pretty efficient operation. We walked down a wooden sidewalk while, at the same time, taking off our clothes and tossing them into specified piles—shirts, pants, shorts, and socks. Then we entered the shower tent, which had plenty of hot water and towels.

After leaving the shower, we walked past the supply boys and shouted out our size. We were then handed the correct items from clothing collected the previous day. During the night, all the dirty duds had been washed and dried. The only item of original clothing we got back was our shoes.

I had a good deal here. My shirtsleeves were longer than average, and the waist and length of my trousers were also not in the normal range. So, when I called out my size, there was no pile of "used" clean clothing. A clerk would have to rummage through the new stock to find me something to wear—usually with the tags still on.

It seems that the tags were considered badges of distinction, and I wore them proudly until they fell off—usually by the time of my next shower.

I remember a few other exciting incidents that happened while we were trying to keep up with the German retreat. There was the day that four of us signalmen were supposed to set up a switchboard a few miles up the road. It was getting dark as we carefully approached a small village. I noticed that all the windows were boarded up, and there were no signs of life.

We held a short conference and decided to spend the night there no matter what. We stopped at the last house in the village and pounded on the door with our carbines. Speaking poor Italian, I shouted, "Open the door, or else!"

An elderly woman, wearing a shawl, cracked open the door and peeked out. As soon as she saw we were Americans, she shouted with joy, threw open the door, and, jabbering faster than I could translate, motioned us into her home.

Including her husband, five grubby-looking partisans were living in the house. As we entered, they reset the safety on their rifles. The partisans were excited at seeing us and began laughing and slapping each other on the back.

They shared their eggs, milk, and vino with us, while we shared our D rations. We got the best of the deal, that's for sure!

The main room in the house was covered with straw, which would give an added cushion to our sleeping bags.

Among the partisans were a twenty-five-year-old tough-as-nails girl and her boyfriend. One member of our switchboard detail (definitely not me) was feeling a little too happy and whispered something in her ear. She quickly ripped the carbine off her shoulder and jammed the muzzle hard against the signalman's stomach. She pulled the bolt back, then forward, and snarled in pretty good English, "Tell me again, soldier, what you would like to do to me tonight!"

The room immediately became quiet. Breathing was rapid. Hearts were pounding. For a moment it was white-knuckle time. Then somebody laughed. The standoff was broken. Once again, everyone started laughing and slapping each other on the back. One thing for sure, we gave the trigger-happy "Annie Oakley" plenty of space that night.

We continued to look around for a spot to set up our switchboard and finally selected a farming community that included a courtyard and several houses. About a dozen families lived here, and they greeted us with cautious exuberance. But when the villagers noticed our troops moving up the road in strength and realized that the Germans would not be returning, every man, woman, and child hurried to the local water well.

We were curious as to what was going on and followed the crowd. The well was about four feet in diameter and had the usual crank and bucket. But that was the only thing typical about this well. Two men with a ladder climbed about ten feet down the shaft and removed a number of bricks from the wall. To our amazement, a large chamber was revealed that contained the villagers' valuable possessions that they had hidden from the Germans.

All the items were carefully laid out in the sun to dry—clothes, farm tools, sewing machines, radios, and other personal property. Their best vino was uncorked, and we partied all night.

By the time the regiment reached the southern end of Lake Garda, the men were tired and exhausted. Then came the news of the German surrender. For the first time, we felt safe from enemy attack. And at mess that evening, there was no dispersement of troops. The men were standing out in the open—like ducks in a pond.

I was busy washing my mess kit in a tub of soapy water when suddenly the scream of a German 88mm shell ripped the air. Everybody hit the dirt. The shell plowed into the ground near me, but there was no explosion. It was a dud. I'll never forget the sound. I can still hear it even after all these years.

A few days later, General Hays called the division together for a job-well-done speech. His back was to the lake, and the troops were facing him. It was mandatory for everyone to attend the ceremony, but a couple of signalmen decided to go grenade fishing instead. I watched their boat move out into the lake. And, as the general was giving his speech, we could see the grenades hit the water and explode without making a sound. Only white plumes of foam revealed what was happening. After about a dozen explosions, the soldiers headed back to shore. They were lucky that General Hays didn't turn around to look at the lake.

I guess a week or two had passed when I was given the job of stringing wire in downtown Riva. One beautiful villa had been draped with about forty telephone lines, and I was adding to the mess.

The madame of the villa was very upset and asked me to move all the wires across the street. I smiled and tried to explain to her that it couldn't be done. But she kept bugging me, and I kept smiling.

Finally, after arguing for several minutes, I lost my cool. I glared at her angrily, adjusted my carbine, and told her that if even one wire was moved or any telephone circuits were lost, the U.S. Army would return the next morning and burn down her villa. Her face turned ashen white and, trembling with fear, she rushed inside the house and slammed the door. She probably thought the wrong side had won the war.

I was one of several signalmen who were granted a week of R&R at Alassio on the Italian Riviera. A buddy and I were billeted at a one-star hotel on a rocky beach. We weren't interested in swimming and decided to climb an adjacent hill to reach the highway and hitch a ride to town.

While climbing the steep slope, I noticed many gun emplacements, tank traps, and rows of barbwire. But we assumed the area was safe. After all, the war was over. However, upon reaching the highway, there were signs all over the place reading, "Keep Out!" and "Uncleared Minefield!"

Alassio was an exclusive enlisted man's town and off-limits to officers. I have often wondered what the officers' exclusive rest-and-relaxation town was like. Unfortunately, that information was never shared.

Just when I thought the war was behind me, the 10th Mountain was ordered to the border of Yugoslavia as a show of force to Marsha Josip Tito. Apparently, he had plans that didn't sit well with the Allied high command.

Tensions were running high. In order to demonstrate a spirit of cooperation, General Hays thought it would be a good idea to show an American movie jointly to both our troops and Tito's soldiers.

Both forces "congregated on the side of a hill to watch the film, starring Alan Ladd. The slope was packed, and every man was armed.

After the movie ended, everybody walked down a pitch-black road to their bivouac areas. Suddenly a shot rang out. A weapon had been accidently discharged. There was a mad rush for cover—the Americans to the left of the road, and Tito's men to the right.

For about sixty heart-pounding seconds, we glared at each other through the darkness, weapons at the ready. Then the standoff suddenly ended. Everyone stood up at once and continued on their respective way. No trigger-happy fingers here!

I didn't smoke and so became a collector of cigarettes. In fact, I had them to burn, so to speak. Every K ration was packed with five cigarettes, and each PX ration included one or two cartons, plus candy bars and peanuts.

I traded my cigarettes for candy, but there is only so much chocolate a guy can eat. It didn't take long before my duffel bag was packed with cigarettes, and I was going home soon. What to do?

A few other nonsmokers were in the same boat, so we got our heads together and came up with a plan. We decided to sell the cigarettes on the black market for twenty bucks a carton.

A little research revealed that the best prices could be had in Rome—a couple of hitchhiking days away. We immediately headed for the big city, taking advantage of various army chow lines along the route.

We had an address, but none of us were experienced with wartime underground activities—or the dangers of going down dark back alleys and knocking on basement doors.

The Italians we were dealing with couldn't speak English—or so they indicated—but it was unnerving the way they watched every move we made.

The black marketeers carefully examined our loot and counted out the negotiated amount in dollars and lira. We were in their clutches, and if they had realized it, we would have settled for an open door to the street. After getting out of Rome alive, we agreed to never do such a thing again.

Once back at our company, we had to convert the lira into dollars before returning to the States. I was also told that I couldn't take home more money than I was paid during my stay in Italy. I knew I had too many dollars and didn't want to have to explain where I got them to a finance officer before boarding a ship for home.

I had no way to spend the extra cash, so I just gave it away. It never dawned on me that all I had to do was claim that I won the money in a poker game. That would have been acceptable.

Just before leaving Italy for the States, I met a fellow from the 34th Infantry Division Signal Corps. He had a German Luger in excellent condition and wanted to trade it for a carton of cigarettes and some candy bars. I knew a good deal when I saw one and kept the pistol hidden until I returned home to the family farm.

I planned to use the Luger to kill rats under the pig feeders and bought a box of 9mm ammunition. But, I soon realized that the cost of bullets per dead rat was about thirty times higher than if I had used .22-caliber rounds. Being smart in economics, I traded the Luger for a run-of-the-mill American-made pistol.

It wasn't long, however, before the price for a German Luger skyrocketed to more than eight hundred dollars, while the value of my pistol remained equal to that of a Saturday night special. Occasionally, I go to gun shows and look at the Lugers—under glass!

CHAPTER 9

Company D, 126th Mountain Engineer Battalion: The Italian Campaign

On April 23, 1945, the 85th, 86th, and 87th Regiments of the 10th Mountain Division began crossing the Po River. Company D, 126th Mountain Engineer Battalion, was attached to the 86th Regiment and manned the assault boats. On April 26, Verona was captured and the 10th Mountain headed for the eastern shore of Lake Garda.

One of the engineers' major projects was the design and construction of an aerial tramway. The specifications required that the equipment could be broken down into sections—weighing no more than 250 pounds each—to facilitate transport by mules or men. The final design looked somewhat like a giant erector set.

The arduous efforts of the Company D engineers contributed significantly to the success of the 10th Mountain Division's rapid advance. In their book The Tramway Builders, *Philip A. Lunday and Charles M. Hampton described the role of the engineers in the Italian campaign. Their story has been edited with permission.*

On January 5, 1945, we boarded the *General Meigs*—supposedly one of America's newest and most modern troop carriers. But this ocean voyage left a lot to be desired.

Boarding was done at night. Evidently, German spies were everywhere. The loading officer called out each man's last name, and after responding with his first name the soldier was permitted to come aboard. But that was the easy part. Just finding our assigned quarters was a bizarre experience. Most of the boys had never been on anything larger than a rowboat.

Sailors directed us into the bowels of this huge floating catacomb. Wearing our helmets and carrying hundred-pound packs, we felt as if it took hours to tread along poorly lit passageways and down steep ladders. Sweating heavily, we were herded like animals into cages.

One section of Company D was escorted four decks down and to the most forward compartment of the ship. The rest of us were packed into the next lower deck, which was below the waterline.

Many of the canvas bunks were next to the hull. This wasn't the best place to spend an ocean cruise, because all rolling and pitching movements of the ship were maximized. Every square inch of space was used. Bunks were stacked six high and about eighteen inches apart.

The heat below decks quickly became unbearable. There would be no air circulation until the engines were going and the ship was moving. To further add to our misery, orders were issued forbidding any soldiers from leaving their assigned space until all the troops were aboard and counted.

The waiting soon became unbearable. Men began throwing up or pissing in their helmets. The fear of being trapped below decks plus the nauseous smells of sweat, vomit, and urine only added to the suffering.

During the whole voyage, motion sickness was the order of the day. Some of the engineers became sick just walking up the gangplank. The mess hall was a couple of decks above the troop quarters. This meant climbing up a grated stairway and past the latrine. The mixture of noxious odors buffeted the men on their way to eat. Early diners, heading back to their quarters, usually lost their meal at the top of the stairs.

Even going to the latrine was an experience. The stalls and urinals were continually in use by the seasick soldiers. One thing was for sure—you always knew what was on the menu before reaching the mess hall.

Enlisted men were served two meals a day. Company D's schedule was early breakfast and late dinner, so that meant we had to wait twelve hours between meals.

The ship rolled and pitched so much that we had to eat standing up while, at the same time, holding on to our trays. Every now and then, someone would throw up and collapse to the deck. After a few days at sea, only the hardiest soldiers were still going to the mess hall—which actually improved the atmosphere aboard the ship.

The officers had their own spacious quarters on the upper deck and were served three meals a day. Their staterooms provided space for four to six men. The nurses and Red Cross girls were also quartered in the same area—enough said! Our only consolation was that the officers got just as sick as the enlisted men.

The ship's crew became the envy of every soldier on the transport. The vessel steamed a regular route from the United States to Europe, then to South America and back to the States. Any luxury items unavailable in the United States or Europe were plentiful in South America—nylons, watches, and cigarettes, in particular. A shipboard black market operated in high gear, and many of the sailors made thousands of dollars trading these items for cash.

After a few days at sea, language lessons in Italian were conducted over loudspeakers. At last, we finally knew our destination. We learned how to ask for the bathroom and say "Please" and "Where can I get some wine?" Other more useful phrases came later.

If there was an oversupply of beer in Italy, it was because of the 10th Mountain Division. When we left the States, our mules were housed on the upper decks of cargo ships, but this made the freighters top-heavy. Apparently, beer makes good ballast, because that's what was used—and plenty of it. The troops had beer coming out of their ears, but not too many complaints. Hard liquor, on the other hand, was in short supply and only rationed to officers.

Only a few soldiers were put to work aboard the ship. Their job was to sweep the decks every afternoon when the call came over the PA system, "Sweepers, man your brooms. Clean sweepdown fore and aft." Ordinarily, you would think this chore would have the same undesirable status as KP. But it quickly became a much sought-after job because the sweepers got three meals a day.

The rest of us, living on two meals a day, were not used to such skimpy rations and thought up ingenious plans to get more food. Chuck Hampton asked Charlie Pruitt—one of the sweepers—how he managed to get into the noon mess. Pruitt showed Hampton his meal pass, which was about the size of a postcard and punched with several holes.

For many of the hungry soldiers, forgery of this card was a piece of cake. The difficult part was faking the punch holes. A pocket knife did the trick. The counterfeits worked so well that half our platoon was soon having lunch every day.

Life aboard ship was routine and monotonous. Immediately after breakfast, the games began—blackjack, poker, acey-deucy, cribbage, and craps.

We had been without an armed escort for most of the voyage, but after entering the Mediterranean we were met by naval vessels.

Our ship docked at Naples, Italy, on January 18, 1945, and we were greeted with our first sight of war. The harbor was littered with sunken ships, while barrage balloons strained at their cables above the dock area.

As the unloading officer called off their names, each soldier staggered down the gangplank where he was met by pretty Red Cross girls offering coffee and doughnuts. Most of the men still had their sea legs, and the ground felt like it was rolling. Some of the guys actually fell down. Others chased the Red Cross girls.

As we marched through the ruins of the city to the rail yard for our trip to Pisa, the men learned a valuable lesson in protecting their belongings. Captain Fred Nagel and Tulsy Davis both had a carton of cigarettes sticking out of a pocket. Ragged young children, darting in and out of our ranks, grabbed the cartons and disappeared in the confusion. The smokes were more valuable than money.

Our next surprise was the sight of the troop train—freight cars with a layer of straw on the floor. In World War I, American soldiers were introduced to the forty-and-eights—boxcars that were supposed to accommodate forty men and eight mules. In this case, however, it was more like fifty and eight. Toilet facilities were either an open door or a crack in the floor.

Every time the train stopped, we were deluged by crowds of desperate Italians bartering or selling anything they thought a soldier might take in exchange for cigarettes or food. There were also pimps hustling for prostitutes and others trying to steal anything they could grab. Some of our men bought wine from the local peddlers but quickly discovered it had been watered down to nothing. We later learned that some of the wine vendors urinated in the bottles to get better color.

When the train made a stop at a town that had bathroom facilities, we got another shock. The toilets were all unisex. They consisted of a wall with a four-foot-wide trough at its base and several open stalls. Ladies selling toilet paper—about the consistency of newspaper—patrolled the stalls.

At Pisa, Company D was bivouacked in a rather pastoral setting. Pup tents were set up in neat rows within view of the famous Leaning Tower. Depressing poverty was evident everywhere. The children were dressed in rags; many without shoes had burlap wrapped around their feet. Most of the young people spoke pretty good English and would sell you their "sister" for a price.

Once we were settled in at Pisa, there wasn't much to do except go sightseeing. Admission to the Leaning Tower was free, so practically everyone took advantage of the attraction. Climbing the winding stairway was a strange sensation. It seemed you were either floating or carrying a hundred-pound weight.

Money had little value here because there wasn't much to buy. A soldier's pay could easily be augmented on the black market. A ten-cent pack of cigarettes could sell for as much as two dollars, and a couple of cigarettes would buy a haircut. Almost anything could be had for smokes.

We were paid in "invasion currency" that was printed in various demoninations of the Italian lira. The bills looked like monopoly money. Authentic Italian currency was practically useless—around a hundred thousand lira traded for one American dollar.

Mail call was the most popular time of day and was usually right after lunch. Relatives and friends of some of the soldiers got pretty clever at sending booze through the mail. A loaf of bread or a cake would be hollowed out to accomodate a bottle of whiskey, and most of the time the package was delivered intact. Of course, there was always the comment, "It looks like so-and-so will be drinking another loaf of bread tonight!"

Around the end of January, Company D moved to Mammiano. We were just over the hill from where our troops and the enemy were dug in. The landscape was desolate. Most of the trees and brush had been cut for firewood. The town had been built on the side of the steep hill and was divided into two sections—up and down. Our company quarters were in a three-story stone house in the lower village, called Mammiano Down. We shared the home with the owners.

Soon after settling into our new lodgings, several of us headed to one of the local saloons. The place was very crowded and smoky. Most of the customers were Americans—armed to the teeth and pretty rowdy. One soldier, from another regiment, made an insulting remark about the 10th Mountain. When he was challenged, the guy pulled out a loaded revolver. For a few moments, I thought we were going to have an old-fashioned western shoot-out. But the MPs quickly arrived, and the pistol-packing soldier quieted down fast—especially when his jaw was broken by a right cross to the head.

Many of the engineers became acquainted with the local residents. One young girl, about fifteen years old, was always coming around with a bucket to collect our table scraps. She took a fancy to a certain soldier and invited him to her home for dinner. The soldier described the interesting evening:

> The house, built of stone, was high on the hill and had a medieval look to it. The walls were bare except for religious objects. The first floor consisted of a sitting room and large kitchen. A fireplace and stove were in the center of the room. There were no logs to burn, just bundles of sticks that had been gathered for firewood.
>
> In addition to the young girl, the family included her mother, grandfather, and a younger boy. The meal consisted of roasted chestnuts and two small fish. As guest of honor, I was offered both fish. Throughout the meal, Mama watched me and her daughter like a hawk. After dinner, the family filled metal pots with hot coals from the fire to be used as bed warmers. When I said my good-byes, everybody shook my hand, and Mama gave me a big hug.

There was supposed to be a veil of secrecy about our arrival. But we were greeted by German loudspeakers welcoming the 10th Mountain to the front. Many of our officers and their units were named—including departure dates from Camp Swift and the names of the troopships. Enemy aircraft dropped propaganda leaflets depicting lewd pictures of our wives and girlfriends in the arms of 4F civilians.

While at Mammiano, we built a tramway as a training exercise and also to check the equipment. The most urgent priority, however, was to zero-in our rifles. This was done before leaving Texas, but with all the bumping around aboard ship, none of us were certain if we could hit what we aimed at.

A small field, approximately a hundred yards long and butting into a hillside, was designated as the rifle range. Targets were set up and carefully measured off. Rifles were sighted at exactly one hundred yards. The range was wide enough to accommodate ten men abreast at a time. Each soldier was issued a clip of eight rounds, which was deemed sufficient to do the job.

Headquarters was the first group to check their sights. They were followed by the first squad of the First Platoon. After half the squad's rounds had been fired and sight adjustments had been made, one soldier—unable to resist the temptation—shot a large green insulator off a nearby power pole that supplied the electricity to Mammiano. The insulator exploded in a shower of pulverized glass. That was the signal for the rest of the squad to join the game, and insulators began popping on every pole.

Frantic screams of "Cease firing! Cease firing, goddamit!" filled the air. Luckily, the power to the village wasn't interrupted, which probably saved the squad from a lengthy tour of guard duty and KP.

Meanwhile, the 10th Mountain was being conditioned to combat situations. Casualties were suffered with increasing frequency. For the previous two years, the Germans had been fighting a largely defensive war in Italy and were masters at the techniques for defending the high ground. The enemy troops had retreated into previously prepared positions in the Apennine Mountains known as the Gothic Line. Perched on the mountaintops, they had held the Allies at bay for three months. Now it was our turn as the 10th prepared for its first major offensive—the attack on Mount Belvedere.

Most of Company D pulled out of Mammiano on February 17. Many of the townspeople came out to say good-bye. Some of them had tears in their eyes. They seemed to know that something was up. As we moved up to the battle line, probes and scouting parties were sent out. Most of the reconnaissance missions were conducted under cover of darkness.

Bob Parker, of the 87th Regiment, led one such patrol and recalled how a Company D engineer saved his life:

We were ordered to scout an area near the village of Corona on the slopes of Mount Belvedere. The path took us right under the nose of the enemy. We crawled or walked in a low crouch and communicated by hand signals or low whispers.

While returning to our lines, my hand brushed a thin wire that ran between my legs. I sent word for an engineer to check it out. Meanwhile, I carefully traced the wire and found it attached to the triggering mechanism of a Bouncing Betty—one of the deadliest booby traps. Even though the night was black as ink, the engineer was still able to disarm the device by feel.

The route of our convoy was across a valley and partway up a mountain that was surrounded on three sides by the enemy. No lights were used by the vehicles. The drivers felt their way along the narrow roadway. If the lead truck had gone over a cliff, the others probably would have followed. Most of us didn't have the foggiest idea of where we were going, and it was probably just as well.

Company D headquarters was set up at Vidiciatico, a small village at the base of Mount Belvedere. Most of the motor pool found shelter in a partially destroyed saloon. One wall was blown out, but the roof was intact. You could actually get high from the fumes of spilled wine. The safest place to sleep was behind the bar. Some of the guys felt right at home there.

Company D's role in the attack on Riva Ridge was to support the infantry with a tramway. Because of the rugged terrain, transporting the wounded to safety would be difficult. The tramway would reduce the evacuation time by up to four hours. In some cases, this would be a matter of life or death. On return trips, the tram would carry ammunition and rations.

Engineering a tramway was difficult under ideal conditions. But, under combat conditions, the task bordered on the near-impossible. First, it was necessary to scout the terrain and find a suitable site. Next, calculations had to be made to prepare the installation and plan of operation. Finally, the equipment and cables had to be lugged in by sheer manpower. And all of this had to be done under the eyes of the Germans, who watched every move from their positions on Mount Belvedere.

At 4 A.M. on February 19, a scouting party under Captain Fred Nagel was sent out to locate a site for the tramway. Available maps, however, proved to be inaccurate. The first site checked was too steep and offered poor anchorage for the main cable. At a second location, the distance was too great for the cables. A site was finally pointed out along the ridge to Mount Cappel Buso—a four thousand-foot peak that faced the west slope of Mount Belvedere.

A survey of the area indicated that a large boulder could serve as the lower anchor. The best spot for the upper terminal was in an orchard about halfway up the ridge. In any event, the tramway would be under continuous enemy small arms and machine gun fire.

At five-thirty on the morning of February 21, the erection of the tramway was underway. It was necessary to clear some brush on the low spots and construct landing platforms at both ends. Trip wires and flares were set in the draws.

On its first day of operation, the tram carried thirty wounded and twenty dead down the mountain. On the return trips, more than five tons of supplies and ammunition were delivered to the troops. The engineers took alternating eight-hour shifts running the equipment. The tram was shut down for two hours each day for maintenance, but no major problems were encountered.

After Belvedere was secured, there was a brief lull in the action. Company morale was high. The temperature was warming up to springlike weather, and the sun was out most of the time.

Company D moved out of Vidiciatico and advanced east to Gaggio Montano. A bivouac area was set up in a large field behind the front lines. Several peaks to the north were still held by the Germans. It was a pastoral setting, and many men didn't dig foxholes. Pup tents were pitched, and everyone relaxed by playing blackjack and other card games.

One morning, just before sunrise, an enemy shell exploded near the mess tent. All the cooks dove into the garbage pit, and one officer was seen crawling out of a muddy culvert under the road. It wasn't a planned attack—just harassing fire by the Germans to let us know they were still nearby. A couple of days later, a shell burst showered us with propaganda leaflets.

On March 3, the Allied forces opened up with an unusually heavy artillery barrage. Specific targets were hit, including German rear-area positions. Our Piper Cub spotter planes directing the artillery fire were flitting around unopposed. The Germans quickly answered the attack with a barrage on our troop concentrations and gun positions.

We stayed in our foxholes anticipating orders to move out at any moment. We didn't have long to wait. The Germans had blown up a strategically located stone bridge. This deprived the 86th Regiment of desperately needed Sherman tank support. Companies B, C, and D of the engineer battalion were immediately ordered to the location. Company C's job was to erect a Bailey Bridge, while Company B was instructed to build a bypass across the stream until the Bailey was completed.

Lieutenant Tom Cole, Company B, brought up an R4 Cat to knock down the riverbank. Rocks were then carried to make a ford so that his men and jeeps could cross. But Cole's company got hit as hard as the bridge builders. It seemed that the enemy gunners had focused in on the noise of the bulldozer.

The Germans seemed to concentrate their attack on the engineers who were carrying packs of TNT, rolls of primacord, Bangalore torpedoes, and C-4 plastic explosive. A direct hit on any engineer would make one hell of a bang.

As our company neared the bridge we noticed three dead engineers. Their bodies had been moved to the side of the road. As Sergeant Hampton recalled, "It was like coming upon a bad traffic accident. My stomach did a flip-flop. I ducked my head and sneaked a look out of the corner of my eye as I walked past the scene."

After the tanks crossed the bridge, we were asked to clear the road of mines. Some of the engineers swept the path in front of the tanks, while others probed the shoulders of the roadway. The men with Bangalore torpedoes remained behind until needed.

We were now in clear view of the enemy. The Germans fired at us with everything they had, but we kept advancing. A minefield was encountered to the right of Mount Terminale. It had been zeroed in by the Germans, and as we entered the area they unleashed an artillery barrage. Despite the heavy shelling, three engineers went out to uncover the mines. But digging was taking too much time. To speed things up, half-pound blocks of TNT were placed on the mines and exploded.

The S mines, or Bouncing Betties, are extremely lethal and very difficult to disarm. They are usually about the size of a large tomato can and filled with small ball bearings. A six-foot wire tether is attached. When the mine is triggered, the can jumps high in the air and explodes, spraying the deadly pellets in all directions. Digging them up required extreme caution and nerves of steel.

As Company D continued its advance, each squad took turns leading the column while, at the same time, looking for signs of disturbance in the roadbed that would indicate the presence of mines. We soon approached a couple of bombed-out farmhouses and a large haystack nearby. As our sweepers moved forward, several well-aimed mortar shells exploded too close for comfort. Chuck Hampton suspected that the Germans had an observation post directing the fire. The shells were falling too close for random shots. The haystack immediately got Hampton's attention, and he told Charlie Pruitt to shoot into the stack. Charlie promptly fired a clip of eight rounds. Sure as hell, three straw-covered Germans stumbled out of the stack with their hands up.

After a brief rest, we came upon a string of about twenty hastily buried Schu mines. The sweepers had uncovered and disarmed a third of them when several mortar rounds bracketed the area. After the barrage lifted, we were joined by a squad from Company C. While discussing the minefield with Sergeant Hampton, the Company C squad leader accidently stepped on a mine. The explosion was deafening. Several men were knocked to the ground and covered with dirt.

When Hampton recovered his senses, the Company C sergeant was lying next to him with most of his right foot missing. Only a blackened heel and ankle bone remained. The platoon medic, Joe Walceski, rushed to help the wounded man. But, suddenly, another flurry of mortar shells pounded the road. Hampton and Walceski covered the injured soldier with their bodies. For a few terrifying minutes, all three men were completely vulnerable—lying prone in the middle of the roadway—waiting for the shelling to stop.

As soon as the enemy barrage ceased, a jeep arrived and the wounded sergeant was quickly on his way to the battalion aid station.

Several minutes later, when the First Platoon rounded a corner, we could see the Malandrone Pass and the 86th Regiment moving along the ridgeline.

Company D followed the infantry advance. As the engineers crossed the ridge, they had a good view of the valley below and a series of meadows and small farms. The infantry deployed across the fields and advanced toward Sassomolari. The Germans still held the village and savagely defended their positions.

On our far left and right, other infantry units were securing the peaks Terminale and della Vedetta. At one point, we took a short break and watched the war—like spectators at a football game.

We soon moved down into the valley and began checking farm buildings for booby traps. One large house appeared to have been a headquarters of some kind. Hampton found an elaborate first aid kit that included a set of surgical instruments. He later traded it for a Colt .45 automatic.

During the rapid Allied advance, the Germans began surrendering in large numbers. As more prisoners were taken, many of our soldiers confiscated their valuables—mainly watches and cameras. One GI showed off his six-inch roll of Italian lira and said he was going to send the money home and buy a new Buick after the war. This, of course, was illegal—but who the hell cared.

By now the front was somewhat stabilized, so most of the engineer battalion returned to road-building jobs. The First Platoon was given the task of repairing Sprilla Road. Sections of the road were nothing more than muddy donkey trails. We installed four culverts for drainage and spread nineteen loads of crushed rock—all this while German shells zoomed overhead.

Sprilla Road curved into enemy territory then looped back to our lines. Therefore, it could not be used as a contiguous supply route. A plan was suggested to build a tramway that would connect both ends of the road that were in American hands.

A careful reconnaissance of the area located an excellent site that ran across a deep gully. Early on the morning of March 11, the Second Platoon began hauling cable through the ravine and up the far side.

About six hours later, a two-thousand-foot cableway was in operation. The tram was soon evacuating more than two hundred wounded men a day—and, on its return trips, carried about thirteen tons of supplies.

Most of the battalion worked on Sprilla Road. The highway had been so poorly constructed that it had to be completely rebuilt. The middle of one stretch of roadway was entirely too high, and the battalion didn't have a grader available. A wrecked German tank, however, solved the problem. The turret was taken apart to make a drag line that was rigged behind a truck. The makeshift contraption worked perfectly, and the road was soon leveled.

The Cat skinners (bulldozer operators) were probably the most overworked and vulnerable soldiers in Company D. When not clearing roads, the skinners were busy digging gun emplacements for our howitzers.

The Cats made a lot of noise that not only drowned out the sound of incoming artillery shells but also attracted them. To counter the threat, a signalman was sent out with each driver to warn of any danger.

One of our company's Cat skinner casualties occurred here. Alvie Allen was out working with his bulldozer when he spotted a bivouac area that had been vacated by the Germans. Lying on the ground in plain view was a highly prized burp gun. As Alvie tried to pick it up, he triggered a booby trap and was blown to pieces.

On another occasion, Rod Rodriguez backed his Cat over a cliff and hit a mine. The explosion blew him off the bulldozer. Luckily, he wasn't injured—in fact, he even landed on his feet. The Cat, however, wasn't so lucky. Mechanics worked around the clock for two days to repair the damage.

Shortly after this incident, some bright officer decided that the Cats should have armored cabs on them to protect the drivers. Sheets of armor plate were collected from supply depots and fabricated into steel covers to shield the tractor operators from enemy fire.

But, as soon as the Cat skinners realized what was happening, they had a fit. The officer who had this brainstorm was told that Rodriguez could have broken his back in such a contraption. The skinners declared in unison that they preferred to take their chances unprotected, and they refused to work under these circumstances. As a result of the protest, no cabs were installed.

The next bright idea suggested was to fit tanks with bulldozer blades. One of the motor pool guys drove one of these modified tanks and said it was pretty spooky. There was only a small slit for visibility, and when the blade was down it was impossible to see where you were going. The Company D skinners thought it was a useless waste of time and money.

Our vehicles were in continual use even though the roads were literally covered with shrapnel. Just keeping up with flat tires was nearly impossible—and getting a truck tire from supply was a major accomplishment. Sergeant Nelson Carver, our chief mechanic, finally solved the problem. He finagled a couple of bottles of booze, requisitioned a truck, and returned with a full load of tires. Word had it that Carver just drove up to the supply depot, handed a guard the package, loaded up, and took off. Sometimes that's how it has to be done in the army.

By this time, our body odors were getting a little strong, so field shower units were set up. Dressing rooms and showers were in tents, but the troops dried off in an open field plainly visible from the road. While standing around in their birthday suits, some of the men were honored by a visit from Clare Boothe Luce, the congresswoman from Connecticut. The naked men didn't seem to shock Luce, but most of the soldiers were embarrassed. No doubt some brilliant general's aid worked out the congresswoman's schedule.

Captain Nagel decided to move our campground to a vineyard on the side of a hill. As it turned out, the bivouac area was under a British five-inch gun battery. They did a lot of night firing, so we had to learn to cope with the noise and sleep with shells flying over our heads.

Several of the engineers became friendly with the English artillerymen. They were crusty characters and spoke with hard cockney accents. Many of us—especially the Southerners—needed translators to interpret what they were saying.

During lulls in the action, field kitchens were erected and warm meals were served. Chicken was the usual fare—probably because the birds could be obtained locally.

We could float nails in the coffee. It was so strong that some of the guys used it to clean their mess kits. After the evening meal, they would fill their canteen cups and mess kits with fresh brewed coffee. By morning, the coffee had turned coal black, and the aluminum mess gear shined like new.

Company D had many of the best cooks in the division and a reputation for serving excellent food. Word got around fast whenever our field kitchen was open for business, and a lot of uninvited guests would always show up at chow time.

Rest leaves were granted for a few soldiers at a time. The destinations, selected by the army, were either Florence or Montecatini. Most of the engineers selected Florence. When the Germans evacuated the city, they blew up all the bridges over the Arno River except the Ponte Vecchio. This bridge was a historic landmark, having been the home of craftsmen during the Middle Ages.

Buildings on both sides of the approaches to the Ponte Vecchio were demolished to block access to the bridge. This seemed somewhat trivial, since the Germans had already stolen as many art treasures as they could carry.

When it was our group's turn to go to Florence, we stayed in a large dormitory type facility. Cots were provided and arranged in neat rows. One night, after lights-out, a violent fight erupted at the far end of the room. It seems that a soldier returned to the dorm in a very intoxicated condition. He stumbled around until he located his cot, then had to relieve himself. In his drunken stupor, what he thought was a urinal was in fact the cot of a sleeping man.

While in the city, most of us ate at Red Cross canteens. Country fried Spam with potatoes was one of the favorite dishes. After all, who wants pasta when you can have Spam!

There were several beer gardens in tthe area, but their offerings were limited. Italian beer was strange stuff when compared with Coors back home. Someone said that the local brew was chemically aged. Judging by its taste, however, it was more like the waste product of an Alpini mule. Grappa, the Italian hard liquor, was everywhere, but some of the street versions were known to have blinded a number of soldiers.

In early April 1945, the Allied armies were spread out along ninety miles of mountainous terrain. A major offensive was planned to jump off on the 13th. Every division had its own strategy, but all had to be coordinated and approved by Corps Headquarters.

One vital element of the attack was artillery and air support. A simple miscalculation would raise havoc with friendly forces. It was expected that some Allied units might advance more rapidly than others. An identification system became of prime importance to prevent mistakes.

First, each company was equipped with yellow smoke bombs to warn off attacking Allied planes. Second, all vehicles were draped with a foot-wide colored banner that was visible from the air.

The 10th Mountain's front was about a mile wide. The 85th Regiment was on the left flank. Its orders were to move down the western slope of Mount della Spe. At the center, the 87th's assignment was to attack the village of Torre Iussi while, on the right flank, the 86th Regiment's mission was to capture Rocca Roffeno.

The engineer companies were divided among the regiments to clear minefields. Because no tramway work was anticipated, Company D was attached to the Third Battalion of the 87th Regiment. This placed Company D at the center of the attack and straddling the Castel D'Aiano Road.

A two-pronged assault was planned, led by companies of the 87th. It was expected that the Germans would permit our troops into the valley but would count on their minefields to slow the advance while their mortars and artillery blunted our attack.

For now, however, the valley—ominously deserted—looked absolutely peaceful. Not even livestock could be seen.

Each squad of our platoon was assigned a specific task, based on the progress of the infantry. As we waited for further orders, weapons were stripped, cleaned, and reassembled several times. But there was always a humorous incident to break the monotony. The First Squad was suddenly sent to division headquarters to dismantle and load General Hays's personal outhouse on a truck.

Then, shortly after midnight on April 14, the night sky exploded. The Allied attack was under way. Flights of heavy bombers dropped more than two thousand tons of bombs on tactical targets. Artillery fire seemed to come from everywhere. The bright flash of explosions lit up the sky. You could read a newspaper by the flash from bursting shells. Sleep was impossible, so we spent the night watching the display of deadly fireworks.

During the bombardment, Captain Nagel received orders to clear the road of mines by 6 A.M. Nagel couldn't believe his ears. "Clear a minefield in pitch black darkness?!"

The dilemma was resolved by the Second Platoon, which began the sweep at daybreak. But that only gave them thirty minutes to clear two hundred yards of roadway.

After several minutes, Captain Nagel realized that the engineers were never going to finish their job in time. Something had to be done. Then an idea hit him. Why not use his jeep as a minesweeper!

The engineers were told to stop their work and get off the roadway. Nagel jumped in his jeep, floored the accelerator, and raced over the road. A series of explosions followed him up one side of the hill and down the other. He never even got a flat tire. Mission accomplished.

Meanwhile, the First Platoon was up at 4 A.M., and after a hot breakfast the men climbed aboard trucks and were driven to the front lines. As they waited for further orders, the engineers spent the time by watching artillery shells zoom overhead. This so-called bomb-watching soon became a common diversion.

About nine o'clock, the platoon moved forward behind the brow of a hill. Moments later, a flight of P-47s roared in low overhead and attacked Rocca Roffeno. The noise was deafening. Empty .50-caliber shell casings rained down on the troops like hailstones.

At exactly 9:45 A.M. our artillery ceased firing, and a couple of infantry companies deployed over the hill. The engineers were then ordered to head down into the valley. After advancing about three hundred yards, an infantry machine gun squad began setting up in the middle of a grove of chestnut trees. We gave them a wide berth. Once the gun was operational, it was sure to attract enemy artillery fire. The machine gunners were to support a rifle company's attack on a group of farmhouses.

Moments later, our howitzers began bombarding German positions. As soon as the barrage lifted, the engineers rushed down the slope and halted in a field. Then the machine gun opened fire. White tracer trails floated across the valley and into the window of a farmhouse. Three Germans scurried out the back door, ducking and dodging among the buildings. They disappeared as the tracers chased them into a small creek.

Chuck Hampton's squad followed a narrow trail toward a possible minefield where a number of unusual mounds had been sighted. They soon came upon two dead Americans sprawled alongside the path.

Hampton suddenly remembered that he had forgotten to take any rations with him. He decided to search the packs of the dead men, but he was interrupted as a mortar shell exploded too close for comfort. The squad quickly scattered, diving into a nearby stream. Three more rounds bracketed the trail—then silence. After waiting several minutes, Hampton and his men climbed out of the water covered with mud.

Chuck hurriedly gathered up three K rations from one of the bodies, then he and his squad continued down the path toward the mysterious mounds. They soon neared a group of farmhouses and the suspicious plot of land. One of the soldiers, with farming experience, immediately solved the puzzle. The supposed minefield was really a vegetable garden, and the small mounds of earth covered a potato crop. They instantly became known as Hampton's "potato mines."

The engineers continued their advance and soon approached Torre Iussi. The village was still occupied by the Germans and was under heavy attack by the 87th Regiment. As Hampton's squad neared a farm building, the body of an American soldier was seen lying near a small crater in the middle of a field. It was obvious that he had been the victim of a mine. A path was cleared through the area and marked with white plastic tape. About twenty Schu and a couple of S mines were uncovered and disarmed.

In the early afternoon, the sweepers stopped to rest at a farmhouse that the 87th had set up as an aid station. It was a busy place, with the medics methodically treating a steady stream of wounded.

As soon as the fighting tapered off, the engineers moved forward to check for booby traps and mines. Hampton's squad suddenly came upon the bodies of several infantrymen from the 87th. Evidently, they had gathered together in a group when a direct hit killed them all. One of the men had been blown in half—body parts were scattered everywhere. The engineers were accustomed to seeing dead soldiers, but the sight of this carnage was very demoralizing.

The main road to Torre Iussi had taken a terrific pounding, and the enemy had blown several large craters in the ground, preventing our Sherman tanks from advancing. A Cat was en route, and Hampton's squad was given the job of setting up a perimeter to protect the bulldozer while the road was being repaired.

Hampton's plan was to position his men between the roadwork and any direct attack by the enemy. The night was unusually dark when the squad moved out to scout the unfamiliar terrain. As the engineers carefully rounded a bend in the road, they saw the smoldering skeleton of a burned-out jeep.

After advancing another hundred yards, the squad came upon three large craters. Hampton checked the vicinity. The land rose steeply to the west and dropped off sharply to the east.

Hampton positioned sentries to the north, south, and west sides of the craters, while he and Charlie Pruitt took the east point and waited for the Cat to arrive.

Chuck Hampton described the frightening night:

> In situations like this, one's senses are tuned to a fine pitch. It's amazing how aware a person becomes at the slightest sound or smell. Eyes play tricks on the mind. A nearby stump takes the shape of a man and even seems to move. We had been taught to use peripheral vision and not to look at an object directly. It usually worked, but not this night. I remember when Pruitt and I both thought we saw something looming in the darkness. We had a long, whispered discussion about whether or not to open fire. But we finally realized that the suspicious object was actually a large rock.
>
> Our nerves had no sooner calmed down than a shadowy figure approached from the direction of the front lines. I softly called out "Halt!" and asked for the password. I never expected the answer "Kamerade!" He was a German soldier who'd had enough of the war and decided to surrender. He will never know how tight our fingers were on the triggers that night—and how close we came to shooting him. There had been several well-reported incidents of Germans approaching our lines with their hands up, only to drop to the ground and start firing.

After the bulldozer arrived, it took the Cat skinner about an hour to fill in the craters. Minutes later, four Sherman tanks rumbled over the patched-up road. Hampton's squad then hurried to Torre Iussi. They reached the village about midnight—dog-tired, hungry, and emotionally drained.

Signal Corps teams were continually busy stringing phone lines, trying to keep up with the advancing infantry. Mules, carrying a roll of wire on each side of their saddles, walked unconcerned, unrolling the wire as they followed their guides.

The engineers were sweeping the area when suddenly—just as the column of mules passed Hampton's squad—a furious barrage of mortar fire bracketed the roadway. Everyone dashed for cover, but the mules just stood there waiting for somebody to pick up the lead rope. None of the mules were hit, but one signalman caught a piece of hot shrapnel in his shoulder.

As the 87th continued its advance, Hampton's squad kept sweeping for mines and booby traps. At one point, the engineers stopped to rest at a farmhouse that was surrounded by the bodies of several enemy soldiers.

It was a short break. Lieutenant John Sheahan came up and gave the squad a new assignment—to clear a possible minefield. The sweep was necessary in order for the infantry to mount an attack on Rocca Roffeno. Hampton's men accomplished the job in about twenty minutes, then took shelter behind a hedge.

The first squad of 87th Infantry Regiment made it safely across the cleared terrain, then all hell broke loose. A barrage of mortar fire plowed up the ground. The Germans, stationed on the high ridges, had the field zeroed in. Two Americans were quickly cut down. A medic hurried to help them but was slugged in the upper arm by a shell fragment.

Hampton looked for a stretcher team. There was none. He rushed into the clearing to help the injured. The wounded medic pointed to the man who had been struck in the hip. Hampton and the medic managed to drag the soldier to an aid station, then hurried back to help the second man, who had suffered a shrapnel wound just above the ear. The soldier was semiconscious and, as he was helped to the aid station, kept repeating, "Mama! Mama!"

By this time, night was approaching and Chuck Hampton's squad returned to the farmhouse. The building was crowded with troops of the 87th Regiment. Their attack had been slowed down, in part because the 85th had been unable to push the enemy back from the high ridges on the left flank. This gave the Germans an unobstructed view of the valley and Rocca Roffeno.

On April 20, the 10th Mountain Division busted through the German defenses and pushed into the Po Valley. As the Allied offensive accelerated, the Americans appropriated anything that would move—cars, trucks, bicycles, and horses. But then, a shortage of brightly colored aircraft identification banners became a major problem. The bunting was cut into smaller and smaller strips until some vehicles had little more than a scrap of ribbon whipping in the breeze. The ribbons were barely visible from the air. And after an 86th Infantry column had been strafed by friendly planes, yellow smoke bombs were used for identification.

The flat terrain was filled with orchards and blooming cherry trees and was perfect for tank maneuvering. Company D stopped at a small farm complex. One of the buildings had been an enemy headquarters. An abandoned hot meal was still on a table.

A short time later, a German truck convoy was sighted heading directly toward our bivouac area. The enemy commander quickly realized his mistake and tried to turn the column around. But it was too late. The convoy was decimated by our artillery and machine guns. This kind of confusion became a common occurrence as the 10th Mountain raced hell-bent across the Po Valley.

Three members of the Company D motor pool had a hair-raising experience while looking for a place to bunk for the night. Bernard Boyd, Tulsy Davis, and Phil Lunday decided to check out a few nearby buildings. They carefully entered a two-story house. Boyd quickly moved upstairs, while Davis and Lunday checked the lower level. The first floor was practically bare of furniture. A sheet was used as a curtain to divide the room. Lunday cautiously approached the sheet and yanked it back. Staring at him was a young German soldier. Neither man was armed, but Lunday was carrying a knife. He nervously tried to pull it from the scabbard while, at the same time, screaming for help. Boyd flew down the stairs with a butcher knife in each hand. The German was scared to death. He was almost as frightened as his captors.

Meanwhile, at the front, the Germans were surrendering in large numbers. Several Company D truck drivers were assigned to haul them to POW compounds in the rear. One driver returned wearing watches stretching from his wrist to his armpits. This doesn't seem like something "good guys" would do, but it was hard to work up any sympathy for the men who, an hour earlier, had been trying to kill us.

Company D's next stop was at Bomporto. Our infantry liberated the town before the Germans could blow up a critical bridge. The span was packed with explosives, and the engineers were called in to remove the danger.

A mess kitchen was set up so we could have a hot meal. But our dinner was continually interrupted by German artillery. Every time a few shells came over, we would hit the deck. Then, after several minutes of quiet, the chow line would re-form—only to be dispersed by another salvo from the enemy guns. It was almost like the Germans were watching and enjoying seeing us scatter. The fun and games went on until the food was cold.

Many of the shells were duds. We could hear the enemy guns fire, then a whistling sound, followed by an explosion or a dull thud. Some shells fell within the company perimeter, but fortunately there were no casualties.

The following day, the Company D engineers climbed aboard trucks and headed for the Po River. Captain Fred Nagel, Al Monroe, and Robert Langner were in a weapons carrier in about the middle of the convoy. The road was very narrow, and Nagel's vehicle had only traveled a few miles when the tailgate popped open. Fixing the problem took longer than expected. By the time the weapons carrier and the trucks behind were able to proceed, the front half of the convoy had disappeared over the horizon.

Nagel and his section hurried to catch up with the other vehicles. But they soon came to a fork in the road. Nagel had to make a quick decision—which path to take. It didn't take long for him to realize he had made the wrong choice. A black German staff car was suddenly seen coming down the road. Nagel realized the potential danger and frantically began to turn his column around—one truck at a time.

The roadway had deep ditches on either side, and turning the trucks in the opposite direction—without them running off the road—was more than difficult. The trucks far in the rear, however, had no idea what was going on. The drivers were startled to see their friends speeding past them the "wrong way."

Tulsy Davis was driving a truck pulling a trailer loaded with an air compressor. Upon reaching the head of the column, he was surprised to see everyone turning around. That's when he sighted a group of enemy soldiers ahead. How Davis managed to turn a thirty-foot vehicle and trailer on a fifteen-foot road is still unclear. But turn it he did, and he began honking and yelling at the trucks ahead to "get out of the way!"

John Warchol and Walter Burns were riding in the headquarter's truck. Warchol was sitting with his rifle across his lap and pointed at Burns. As they bounced around in the vehicle, the firing pin on Warchol's rifle clicked. Warchol took the bullet out of the chamber, looked at it, remarked "dud," and tossed it aside. At the next stop, a visibly pale and shaken Burns changed trucks.

Company D finally reached the Po River near the town of San Benedetto. A bivouac area was set up near the main highway that crossed the river. All bridges had been destroyed, and the officers were busy trying to figure out how to get across. Our supply lines were already stretched to the limit, and the assault boats still hadn't arrived. General Hays was fuming mad at the delay.

Late in the afternoon, a large German convoy was observed moving toward the intersection of the two main highways. We deployed four tank destroyers in a grove of trees and laid in wait for the enemy.

As the German column approached our lines, it was recognized as a heavy artillery battery looking for a way to cross the river. The lead enemy vehicle was pulling a huge gun—probably a 170mm howitzer. A couple of warning shots were fired at the convoy. The Germans immediately answered with machine guns.

From there on, it was complete carnage. All four tank destroyers blazed away at once. The destruction was amazingly swift. Three soldiers in the lead vehicle were burned to a crisp. An American sergeant appeared from nowhere and ended up in a ditch with the top of his head blown off. When the shooting stopped, dozens of the enemy littered the ground.

Panic must have gripped the Germans in their hurry to cross the river before the bridges were blown up. The south shore of the Po was cluttered with abandoned vehicles and equipment. One bus was packed with musical instruments belonging to a regimental band. Another vehicle contained several thousand Italian lira—probably counterfeit.

A few Company D soldiers picked out some German staff cars to drive around in. They were having a lot of fun until someone reminded them that Allied aircraft searched out the staff cars for target practice.

Company D received two assignments for the Po River crossing. One section was detailed to man the assault boats when they arrived. Another group was designated to erect a tramway over the Po.

A scouting party was sent out to check a small island in the river that might provide an anchorage for the tram. The scouts had no sooner splashed ashore than a fierce artillery barrage pounded the island.

At first, Captain Nagel believed that the Germans had zeroed in on the island—then he realized that the bombardment was coming from our own guns. He quickly stopped the shelling but feared his men were all dead. He was relieved when they began popping up one at a time from several caves on the island. Not one soldier was even wounded.

As soon as it became dark, the tramway detail set out to begin work. The men climbed aboard a truck that also pulled a trailer loaded with the tramway motor. A full moon illuminated the terrain. Just as the truck reached the main road to the river, a German fighter plane appeared. The pilot had spotted the vehicle and raced in with guns blazing. Lieutenant Bob Martin shouted for the driver to stop so that his men could bail out. Enemy tracers plowed up the ground in front of the truck.

The engineers scattered like a covey of quail to whatever safety they could find. Sergeant Chuck Hampton dove under a barbed wire fence and lost the back of his pants. The enemy aircraft made two more passes, then sped away.

A nearby Sherman tank fired a few machine gun rounds at the plane, and there were some rifle shots. But overall, the counterattack was somewhat pathetic.

A few minutes later, the tank driver stopped by our truck for a brief chat. He had liberated a case of schnapps and gave a bottle to the engineers. It proved to be just what the doctor ordered. After a short delay, the tramway crew again headed for the river—this time slightly fortified.

Meanwhile, the 10th Mountain troops were chomping at the bit waiting to cross the Po—but the assault boats still hadn't arrived. It was then that the engineers pulled off one of the great scams of the war.

The original plans for crossing the river called for the 85th Infantry Division (not to be confused with the 85th Regiment) to get the landing craft and be the first outfit to reach the far banks of the Po. This decision didn't sit well with General Hays. In his opinion, since the 10th Mountain was the first division to reach the river, it should be the first across.

After giving the problem some thought—and becoming angrier by the minute—Hays decided on a swift course of action. He told Major Platt Boyd and several other officers to search the rear areas for any boats they could find.

Warrant Officer Heller lucked out. He came upon a truck convoy hauling about fifty landing craft destined for the 85th Division. Heller was a smooth talker, and he convinced the convoy commander that he could escort the trucks to the division's location.

By this time, it was late in the day and would soon be dark—a perfect time for what Heller had in mind. He led the convoy to the 10th Mountain's position on the river.

It was after midnight when the trucks reached the Po, and everybody turned out to unload the boats. By the time the convoy commander realized what was happening, it was too late. The landing craft were at the water's edge, and the truck convoy was on its way back to where it came from.

The Germans had fortified their side of the river. They were determined to stop the relentless Allied advance, and they put up a strong resistance. Enemy artillery shells were set to burst just above the water and directly over our staging areas.

Company D provided three-man crews for the boats that carried a dozen infantrymen each. Captain Nagel went across with the first wave to scout the far shore. The troops took cover in an abandoned dugout and captured a German soldier. The prisoner wondered why we weren't fighting alongside the Germans against the Russians. He remarked, "Just wait, they'll be your enemies before long!"

Chuck Hampton, Charlie Pruitt, and Ray Cleverly were the crew of a boat in the second wave. Feeling vulnerable was normal for men crossing a river only two hundred yards wide while under enemy fire. For the troops sweating out the ride, however, the short trip seemed to take an eternity.

One soldier, tired of being a sitting duck, suddenly began using his rifle butt as a paddle. Moments later, every man aboard the craft was paddling like crazy. As the boat neared the far shore, an enemy shell exploded overhead. Flying shrapnel ripped the landing craft. A soldier was hit and tumbled into the water. Weighted down by his pack, he was in danger of drowning. Hampton recalled:

> I managed to grab a shoulder strap of his field pack. We were still underway. I dragged him along until we were about twenty yards from the beach, then I jumped into the river and pulled him ashore. He had caught a piece of shrapnel in his thigh, but it wasn't a life-threatening wound. As he was sputtering and spitting river water, I asked if he wanted a return trip. He looked at me like I must be crazy and answered between coughs, "Not on your life! I'll take my chances over here!"

The engineers made from six to eight round trips, and by the time all the troops had crossed the Po, only ten boats were still afloat.

On April 25, the engineers completed a pontoon bridge, and a flood of tanks and heavy equipment began rumbling over the temporary span. This was the only river crossing for miles, and the world's greatest traffic jam quickly developed as hundreds of vehicles impatiently waited their turn.

The Company D Cats were loaded on large flatbed trailers and interspersed among the trucks and jeeps. Division MPs were busily directing traffic. This was the first time any of us had ever seen them do anything. But they probably had their hands full trying to figure out what to do with the hundreds of surrendering Germans.

Captain Nagel led our company across the Po. Each truck driver had strict instructions about spacing the vehicles so that the bridge didn't sink from the weight. Only one Cat-carrying truck was allowed on the bridge at a time. But, even so, the pontoons heaved up and down like a ship in rough seas. A few engineers were stationed on the pontoons in case adjustments had to be made to the anchor lines. But nobody felt safe until they had crossed the bridge and reached dry land.

The army's attack strategy, north of the Po, called for the infantry regiments to leapfrog each other. But our troops were moving so fast that the regiments had trouble keeping up with each other. The 10th Mountain had very little mechanized equipment, so General Hays issued an order for his division to commandeer anything that moved.

The word spread like wildfire, and the 10th Mountain columns soon began to include horses, oxcarts, motorcycles, bicycles, and automobiles. One enterprising soldier, tired of riding a horse, swapped it with a farmer for a large wooden cask containing twenty-five hundred gallons of wine. After his friends loaded up all they could carry, he posted a sign on the farmhouse inviting everyone to share his good fortune. The Company D engineers also participated in the happy event and managed to liberate a considerable quantity of the grape.

As we entered the small towns and villages, our welcome was often quite moving. The roads were lined with cheering throngs. Lots of kisses were exchanged with the local girls—and some of the grandmothers, too! Hidden kegs of wine appeared from nowhere, and most of our five-gallon water cans were quickly filled with vino. The mood was festive. Everybody was happy.

Despite the heartfelt welcome from the civilians, we proceeded with caution. Machine guns were at the ready, pointed at second-story windows and other potential enemy hiding places.

Tactically, the 10th Mountain Division was completely surrounded by Germans. About halfway to Verona, our columns came to a complete halt. Word had been passed that a large body of enemy troops was approaching us from the west. Captain Nagel ordered machine guns set up in a large drainage ditch, and infantry was deployed along the bank. We sweated it out a couple of hours until the emergency was cancelled—without a German soldier being sighted or a shot being fired.

A short time later, we had just captured a railroad station when a fully loaded enemy troop train pulled into the depot. Nagel didn't know what to expect and had to think fast. He told the station master to have all the German officers come to the building. Nagel then confronted them through an interpreter. At the same time, our men were ordered to slowly appear from their hiding places along the tracks. It was a perfectly choreographed operation and averted a potential gun battle.

When Company D reached Verona, the city didn't resemble what you would expect as the home of Romeo and Juliet. Before the war, it had been a major rail center but was heavily bombed and almost totally destroyed. Fires were burning and smoldering everywhere, and the terrain was pockmarked with bomb craters.

One of our squads came upon three enemy soldiers who climbed out from a culvert and surrendered. The squad's sergeant, while searching one of the prisoners, pocketed the German's Omega watch. A new second lieutenant whom nobody recognized saw what happened. The officer was pretty upset, and chastised the sergeant, reminding him that confiscating the personal property of a prisoner was against the Geneva Convention.

The sergeant took as much of the chewing-out as he could stand then demanded to know—in no uncertain terms—just what kind of war the lieutenant thought he was fighting. The sergeant angrily pointed out that if he returned the watch, some rear echelon bastard would grab it. The admonished lieutenant finally decided that the sergeant could keep the watch.

The following day, the 10th Mountain was ordered to move as fast as possible to Lake Garda. Thousands of retreating Germans could be trapped by cutting off their escape route into the Alps.

As we hurried north out of Verona, the sounds of heavy fighting could be heard in the distance. Near the outskirts of town, a major German ammunition depot exploded, the huge mushroom cloud nearly blocking out the sun.

On April 28, the 10th Mountain reached Lake Garda and began moving up the east side. We were all very tired and dirty, but the scenery was spectacular with a view of the Alps towering above the lake. The mountains were awesome—like nothing most of us had ever seen before. Storm clouds seemed permanently attached to the summits, and sheer cliffs dropped almost straight down to the water's edge.

The highway to the resort city of Riva was cut through tunnels of solid rock and traversed bridges and trestles. This made it easy for the Germans to block the tunnels and stall the 10th Mountain's advance.

Duels between our artillery and the German guns were continuous. Most of our effort was concentrated on the town of Torbole at the north end of the lake.

Over several years, the Germans had tunneled into the granite cliffs of Mount Brioni, which gave them a commanding view of almost everything from Torbole south.

If the 10th Mountain was to continue its momentum, an amphibious operation would be necessary. Every kind of small craft imaginable was assembled to carry the infantry, and barges were commandeered to haul artillery and tanks.

Company D was put immediately to work. A number of men were assigned to the boat crews, while other engineers were given the job of building a ramp so that tanks could be loaded aboard barges and ferried around the tunnels. A shallow location on the lake was picked for the project. Large logs were lashed together with tramway cables to make a serviceable ramp. The engineers worked in waist-deep cold water, but there were few complaints—it was their first bath in weeks. However, driving the initial Sherman tank over the ramp was a real nail-biter. The tank's captain was hesitant to test the contraption, but it held together—much to everyone's relief.

A couple of engineers were assigned to each barge, and "ducks" were used to tow the flat-bottom boats. The night was totally black when the first tank-carrying barge moved cautiously into the lake. The "duck" operators had to rely on the engineers for course directions. Instructions were delivered by the engineers running back and forth across the decks shouting their orders.

As the barge neared its destination, the "ducks'" motors were cut, and hauling lines were tossed to men on the shore. Unloading the tanks, however, was another matter. The only kind of ramps available were wooden footbridges that the infantry had used in disembarking from the small boats.

As Captain Nagel recalled: "I remember one tank coming off the barge and just grinding the ramp into toothpicks. I thought sure that the tank would drop right into the drink. But somehow the cleats caught hold and it rumbled ashore."

A short time later, tanks and trucks began arriving on motorized barges. Several of the flat-bottom boats were bolted together, and an engine was installed with the help of a crane. One of our mechanics rode along for emergencies.

Meanwhile, clearing the tunnels of debris was a sickening job for the Cat skinners. When the entrance to one tunnel was unblocked, a truck with several dead German soldiers inside was discovered. Evidently, explosives set to blow up the tunnel had detonated prematurely. The bodies had partially decomposed, and the stench of death was almost unbearable.

Reopening the road was a monumental task, and the crews worked around the clock. Colonel John Parker, commanding our engineer battalion, was fired by General Hays when he told the general that it would take five days to clear the road. This wasn't fast enough for Hays, and he blew his stack. But despite the good general's demands, the work still took five days.

When the road was finally opened for traffic, Company D was quartered in a beautiful old villa overlooking Lake Garda. The house was owned by an aging opera singer. On the second floor of the residence was a music room with a large grand piano and shelf after shelf of sheet music. One wall was covered with signed photographs of the lady in company with distinguished-looking people. We believed that one of the photos pictured her with a young Arturo Toscanini.

The room was furnished with comfortable chairs and lounges. It probably had been used for intimate gatherings of music lovers and opera buffs. I often wondered what the lady must have thought of having to put up with a bunch of dirty, coarse, barbarian Americans.

One afternoon, our hostess—who was of heroic Wagnerian proportions—decided to give us bums some culture. She proceeded to sing a few selections from operatic arias. Bob Cochran sang the respondent part of the ballads. Then, Chuck Hampton treated us to an operatic melody that he played on a captured coronet.

Although we didn't know it at the time, this romantic villa proved to be the end of the war for Company D. But there were still pleasant surprises. Company K, of the 87th Infantry, discovered several large caves near the Swiss border that had been stocked with French champagne and cognac.

When General Hays learned of the find, he had the plunder sent to our division supply depot, and the bottles were divided among every company. Fifty-five truckloads were needed to empty the caves, and the engineers supplied most of the vehicles and manpower. It was definitely a labor of love.

During the Italian campaign, Company D erected two tramways under combat conditions—a first in American military history. But probably the greatest tribute accorded the 10th Mountain Division was the recognition by professional German officers, who praised the 10th as an elite corps of soldiers.

CHAPTER 10

The 10th Mountain Cavalry Reconnaissance Troop: The Italian Campaign

The strangest organization attached to the 10th Mountain Division was the 10th Mountain Cavalry Reconnaissance Troop. The unit was originally formed at Fort Meade, South Dakota, as a horse cavalry outfit.

In November 1942, the troop was sent to Camp Hale, Colorado, for winter training. It was hoped that the men might be able to maneuver equally on horses and skis. However, this was not the case. Consequently, officers and men of the troop were split up among various quartermaster companies. They were then replaced by expert mountaineers and the horses were replaced with mechanized equipment.

The troop's mission was also changed. The men became instructors, teaching rock climbing to 10th Mountain soldiers at Camp Hale and glacier techniques at Mount Ranier, Washington.

In the autumn of 1944, the Cavalry Reconnaissance Troop was reactivitated at Camp Swift, Texas, and soldiers with horse experience were transferred into the outfit.

Donald Hubbard recalled his experiences with the "Horse Cavalry" in Italy.

After arriving at Naples, we moved inland and were billeted at San Marcello. We received jeeps (no horses yet) and began reconnaissance patrols into the mountains and high ground occupied by the Germans.

In the spring, we were trucked to Florence where we would finally receive our mounts. This good news lifted our spirits and gave us something different to talk about, such as what their color might be or their size, age, and temperment.

Our first look at the horses, however, was somewhat disappointing, as they seemed very docile. We learned that they had been obtained from the French, Sardinians, Hungarians, and Germans. A two-day ride to the front revealed that our evaluation of the horses was correct. But then maybe it was better to have mounts that were easy to control, especially under fire.

On April 14, 1945, the Po River campaign began, with the 10th Mountain heading the attack. The division rushed ahead so fast that the enemy was unable to establish an effective defense.

As mounted cavalrymen, we still didn't have riding boots or spurs, but that didn't deter us. Our horses stood up well to the attack, but they often lacked the correct diet. The Italian people, however, often came to our rescue with whatever food they could spare.

Our objectives were not always clear, but part of the confusion was due to the large number of Germans who were surrendering. Our instructions were to send the prisoners to the rear. Other orders were to bypass pockets of resistance.

It was at one of these so-called pockets of resistance that the Cavalry Reconnaissance Troop fought one of the strangest battles of the war.

We had advanced within a few kilometers of the Po River when we came upon a small Italian village. The troop was moving in formation, single file with the First Platoon in the lead. There were buildings on a side street to our left, giving us a choice of either going straight ahead or turning left and passing in front of the buildings.

The decision was quickly made for us. German machine guns, on the second floor of a stone dwelling, opened fire on our troops. The Third Platoon commander ordered a pistol charge on the enemy position, but some of his men were unarmed.

The First and Second Platoons dismounted and prepared to support the assault. What the Third Platoon lacked in firepower was more than made up for by its overabundance of courage. Our supporting volleys were able to suppress the enemy guns, giving the Third Platoon a chance to recover and withdraw. The pistol charge was unsuccessful but ended without casualties to men or horses.

The use of horses in this campaign ended when we reached the Po River at San Benedetto. We tied our horses in an orchard of fruit trees, bid them farewell, and crossed the river in boats.

CHAPTER 11

The Diary of a German Soldier

The following excerpt from a POW German officer's diary was printed in the March 18, 1945, issue of Stars and Stripes. *John Dewey's edited version appeared in his booklet* Fecit.

As Dewey commented, "This German officer was captured during our recent attack northeast of Mount della Torraccia. Filled with bitterness and despair, the diary is typical of the mood that prevailed at this time among German soldiers fighting on the Italian front."

While reading this account, however, two things should be kept in mind. First, the writer—while fully realizing the hopelessness of Germany's situation—nevertheless continued to do his duty. Second, this same officer, who in 1945 discovered that war was terrible, would hardly have had the same opinion in 1940, when the German Army was rolling practically unopposed across Europe.

February 13, 1945

Time flies. Forever boring! What great deeds can one put into a diary? "All Quiet on the Southern Front" as Erich Remarque (author of *All Quiet on the Western Front*) would say. Mail from Gertrude. She has not received any mail from me in two months. An inspection of our position revealed one man dead and one wounded. The high command news report did not mention this.

One thinks about the war, and of the future. Do we have any future at all? I start philosophizing. But what good is Schopenhauer's philosophy, Goethe's *Faust*, Nietzsche's "superhuman being," and Fichte's well-meant speeches? All of us, whether young or old, officer or enlisted man, are subject to the laws of this embittered war. Its iron fist sends us scurrying into the smallest holes whenever the steel splinters start flying. Every time the Yankee pulls the lanyard, we become like hunted animals. Every survival instinct is put to use. This is war, but in such moments, it loses all of its glory.

Karl von Clausewitz wrote, "War is the father of all things." But why are we soldiers unable to grasp the hidden meaning in these words? And why are we, who must live through the last murderous phase of this war, considered so loathsome? Perhaps wars, in all their terrible bitterness, are tests for the small, ugly, and cruel humans.

But then, perhaps, the helmet-crowned graves of the dead from all nations call out for the truth to be heard. In the words of God, "Peace on Earth, and good will toward men." Burn these words deep into your hearts, you men of all nations. War! Never again! Now leave me in peace with my tormenting thoughts. I am of good will, but I also have German blood in my veins. I only do what I believe to be my duty.

February 20, 1945

Yesterday we fired some shells into Poretta. This must have made the enemy feel very uncomfortable, as shortly thereafter he began a mighty show of fireworks on Pietra Colora.

On the right, the Americans are again reported to have penetrated our positions. Since seven o'clock this morning, their fighter bombers are continually humming in the sky above us, and their machine guns are hammering without letup.

The other side knows as well as we just how much the wheat fields of the Po Valley mean to us. Gertrude writes that Prisdorf has suffered heavily. She would rather wait a little longer before getting married. Women are funny. One will not wait for you because it takes too long, and another wants to wait longer. Well, I won't talk about that anymore.

February 23, 1945

It's 8 P.M. The entire area is alive with explosions. The bunker is shaking. Carbide lamps are blown out, and pressure is exerted on our ears. I hope nothing has happened to the food truck.

Last night, I was out scouting until five in the morning. I now have more details on the enemy's penetration. Mount Belvedere, Mount della Torraccia, and Mount Castello are now in American hands. One of our regiments is almost completely destroyed. Two companies have gone over to the enemy.

February 25, 1945

After a quiet morning and afternoon, all hell has broken loose this evening. Explosions everywhere. One of our regiments is fleeing in disorder. A staff sergeant, whom I had visited only three days ago, has been captured with two of his squads.

Then, just now, a man from the retreating regiment reported that I'll have to pull back my outpost. I moved to the old platoon command post at Pietra Colora. I could not observe the enemy from here, but if we don't counterattack soon, we will all end up as prisoners of war in places like Canada or Kansas. If my darling only knew what filth I am sitting in!

February 26, 1945

The night passed quietly. I am now in the first platoon command post. The sky is alive with enemy planes. And we just have to sit here patiently and take it. I could cry in the face of all this enemy superiority. We cannot show ourselves during daylight. That would be suicide. One's nerves must be made of steel to stand here. It borders on the superhuman. May the end be at least halfway bearable for my Germany!

February 27, 1945

Today, once again, I barely escaped death. We were on the right flank. The Yankees must have seen us as we sprinted across a moonlit yard. A rain of bullets followed. I hugged the ground and crawled to the corner of a building. Suddenly there was a terrible explosion. I heard a cry for help. One of our men was seriously wounded. His left thigh had been ripped off, and he had shell splinters in his belly.

War is horrible. Anyone who has never been through it—especially as an infantryman—can't possibly picture what one human can do to another. We are constantly hurling death and destruction at each other. Damned humanity! What insanity you are committing!

My sweet darling, if you only knew what terrible fears I have. I only hope that we will be out of here sometime soon.

March 2, 1945

My nerves seem to be calmed. Things have quieted down during the last few days. Our position is considerably better now. The Yanks no longer look straight down our throats. Our men stay in their holes during daylight hours, but due to the damn planes they can't move about.

Three sergeants and two privates have disappeared during our disengaging movement. I wonder if they deserted. Anything is possible. There are times when we soldiers get pretty downhearted. Even I have had just about enough.

The regiment to my right will be relieved tonight. I wonder if we too—in the course of time—will be moved to the rear. In five more days we will have been on the front lines for four months without relief. Our losses so far are not particularly heavy—which is probably why we have been kept here so long.

CHAPTER 12

The Italian Campaign: A German Retrospect

In his book, The German Army in the West, *published in 1951 by Cassell & Co., Ltd., General Siegfried Westphal described the problems of defending Italy against an invasion by Allied forces during World War II.*

The Italian peninsula has the longest coastline of any European country. And neither this long sea-flank nor the offshore islands have natural defenses of any consequence. The only exception is a stretch of about 120 miles on either side of Genoa. Practically everywhere else, an enemy landing could be made without too much difficulty.

Permanent defenses—constructed in peacetime—were few in number and were concentrated around naval bases. Also, the resources of men and material were inadequate for building permanent fortifications, even at strong points. In any case, where should these fortifications have been built along a coastline of two thousand miles, with its many possible landing sites?

It is the attacker who has the option of landing where he believes the prospects of success are the best. The defender can only guess as to the enemy's intentions. If the defender guesses correctly, he can distribute his forces so that some units can launch a counterattack at the moment the enemy comes ashore.

It is also necessary to be able to move reserve forces quickly so they can be hurriedly summoned to danger-points. And, it goes without saying that all troop movements must be covered by antiaircraft guns and fighter aircraft.

The country of Italy south of the Po Valley is mountainous and offers excellent prospects of slowing down an enemy advance—if not stopping it altogether. This same kind of terrain, however, precludes a highly developed transportation network. Therefore, the only dense railway system is located in the northern part of the country.

Three rail lines thread south through the mountains. Two of them have double tracks as far as Naples. The third becomes a single track line just south of Ancona.

All the railroad tracks cross a number of rivers and valleys—with many bridges, viaducts, and tunnels. The entire railway system was extremely vulnerable to air attacks, particularly since the trains were largely electrified.

The western and eastern rail lines run along the coast and were easily threatened from the sea. The network is thinnest in the south, and only a few bombing raids could put it out of action for a considerable period of time. Even in the center of the country, the destruction of only a few bridges could cripple rail traffic for weeks.

Roads and highways, however, were in much better shape. But, although they had been extended over a period of years, the numerous steep grades and easily blocked mountain roads crippled the rapid movement of troops.

Because of the difficulty in defending the country against invaders, Italy was at the mercy of an attack from the sea. Also, the transportation of practically all goods was more the job of coastal shipping than the rail lines or highways.

Before the war, Italy's merchant marines were able to safely carry every kind of cargo to any port on the peninsula. But, Allied mastery of the Mediterranean almost paralyzed this kind of traffic. Although the railroads attempted to take over the task, they were unable to do so. The delivery of food supplies to the civilian population soon became a serious problem and led to an alarming rate of undernourishment, especially in the southern part of the country.

When one realizes that Italy is almost entirely lacking in raw materials such as iron, coal, and oil that are indispensable for waging modern war, it can be readily appreciated that the nation's leaders had an enormously difficult task.

Field Marshal Albert Kesselring believed that the absence of German naval forces—and the weakness of the Luftwaffe—would enable the enemy to make a major amphibious landing in the vicinity of Leghorn without significant impediments.

If they were successful, the Allies would be able to block the passes of the Apennines before the German divisions—moving on foot—could reach the invasion site. This attack could bring about the collapse of our forces in the south.

But even a landing closer to the front lines would soon require our troops to retreat, because we had insufficient forces to defeat both a landing and a frontal assault.

Of particular worry was the fact that hostile aircraft would not be greatly hindered by the weather. Therefore, it became almost impossible to move men and supplies during daylight hours.

Regarding our strategy in Italy, nearly all the German soldiers were experienced in battle and generally adequate for the defensive tasks assigned to them. The Luftwaffe, on the other hand, had been almost entirely driven from the sky and was unable to render assistance. Our naval forces were completely absent, and the number of U-boats and other craft was comparatively insignificant. The main burden of the war, therefore, was carried by the German land forces. They would have been better able to bear it if they had been provided with adequate supplies of ammunition, food, and medical aid.

We were always short of ammunition and were scarcely ever able to equal the enemy's rate of fire. There was also a severe shortage of petrol, spare parts, and warm clothing. Even the meager supplies delivered to us did not always reach the front regularly.

The enemy's air force attacked the rail lines day and night—as weather permitted—so that it was impossible to tell when our supplies, coming down from the north, would reach the frontline troops.

Many hours were spent working out new expedients to ease our difficulties. Improvisation was the daily bread of the German high command. It was characteristic of the "poor man's war" that they were forced to conduct.

The overall war situation deteriorated in 1943 and became even worse the following year. The heavy casualties, the loss of many sources of raw materials, and the increasing effect of enemy air power made it difficult to recruit personnel and to provide weapons, ammunition, and fuel.

After the spring of 1944, the German high command found it increasingly hard to satisfy even the modest requirements of the Italian theater. This front became of secondary importance compared with the western front. It was even necessary to deprive Kesselring of several veteran divisions and cut down his supplies.

At first, Hitler had allowed his commanders in Italy limited freedom of action. However, after the Allied landing at Anzio, he began to intervene more drastically. Our commanders were now continually pestered with trivialities and numberless details. Hitler prescribed answers to all sorts of questions that could only be properly decided on the spot.

It is true that Kesselring enjoyed Hitler's favor to a certain extent and had a knack that often enabled him to get his own way. There was, of course, another factor whose psychological effect must be acknowledged. Kesselring wore the uniform of the Luftwaffe and therefore in Hitler's eyes was not as "prejudiced" as the army commanders.

Although this made Kesselring's job easier, Hermann Göring, Commander of the Luftwaffe, missed no opportunity to blacken the field marshal's name. Regardless, the steadfastness of our army officers could not fail to be affected by the intervention of the high command and by Hitler's wakeful suspicions that something was being hidden from him—that an order had not been carried out, or that a favorable opportunity had not been exploited.

This incessant occupation with all kinds of details—which was intensified by Hitler's daily questionings—often made it difficult to see the forest for the trees. The continual demand that the impossible be made possible hindered our strategic efforts.

Our army group constantly struggled with the tendency to become too hesitant in its actions. In fact, by accepting the risk presented by the long sea-flank, it may have overstepped the limit of boldness.

The army group knew full well that a successful enemy landing would mean the end. But the important thing in the group's mind was to keep Allied air bases as far away as possible from the south German sky. In this respect, the troops succeeded. The enemy never did attempt a daring airdrop behind the German lines.

In Africa, the main burden of the struggle did not fall on the shoulders of the army until the autumn of 1942, but in Italy the army bore the brunt of the fighting right from the beginning. Our hopes were nourished by communications from the Luftwaffe high command that we would receive modern fighter aircraft in large numbers by early summer of 1944 at the latest. This promise was not fulfilled. An Italian general was right when he told me in August 1943, "The Wehrmacht can send as many divisions to Italy as it likes, but if the Luftwaffe is not strengthened, a hundred divisions will not be able to hold their own."

The fighting abilities of the Allies were fairly even. Their weapons and equipment, however, were generally excellent, and they were more amply provided with tanks than the Germans.

The enemy's numerical superiority made possible regular relief of its forces as well as the formation of a strategic reserve. The Allies' supply system was unsurpassed because the sea lanes were open, while our railways never were.

The Allied naval and air units possessed absolute supremacy, and the cooperation between the various branches of the armed forces appeared to be exemplary. On the German side, the army group commander could only "request" support from the Luftwaffe and the navy. The chain of command was much more clearly defined among the Allies. Field Marshal Sir Harold Alexander was a *real* supreme commander equipped with all necessary powers, not a shadow-king like Kesselring. Alexander received his assignment, reported his intentions, and, after their approval, was free to carry them out in the way he thought best. No one meddled in the details of his actions.

All the prerequisites for victory were therefore present on the Allied side. If the defeat of their German opponents took a great deal of time, this was probably due to an attitude of "safety first."

If, in September 1943, the Allies had landed not at Salerno but near Rome—and in January 1944 not at Anzio but near Leghorn—it would have cost them fewer casualties. This cautiousness caused them to miss other opportunities. But, in the end, the Allied victory came from a frontal attack, after the troops had gnawed their way from the toe of Italy's boot and up the leg.

The Allies certainly could have captured the southern and middle section of Italy as early as the autumn of 1943 by a large-scale enveloping movement. It is also impossible to dispute that a landing near Leghorn in early 1944 would almost certainly have cut off Kesselring's army group.

We had nothing in the Po Valley that could be called "soldiers." The entire Apennine peninsula could have been in Allied hands by the summer of 1944. The German weak points were quite apparent to the Allies. They knew that the Luftwaffe had been driven from the skies, and they knew the difficulties we were having in supplying our troops and how short we were on reserves. Their desire to take as little risk as possible prevented the Allies from bringing about a quicker decision to the conflict.

The Allies gained rich military experience in the Mediterranean theater—particularly in the art of amphibious warfare. This knowledge formed the foundation for the planning and execution of the Normandy invasion in 1944. The same held true for the development of the Allied armed forces as a whole. The former system of planning land, sea, and air warfare separately now made way for closer cooperation. From now on, the sea is a roadway like any other—for the one who commands it.